1,000,000 Books

are available to read at

www.ForgottenBooks.com

Read online
Download PDF
Purchase in print

ISBN 978-1-330-15915-6
PIBN 10040582

This book is a reproduction of an important historical work. Forgotten Books uses state-of-the-art technology to digitally reconstruct the work, preserving the original format whilst repairing imperfections present in the aged copy. In rare cases, an imperfection in the original, such as a blemish or missing page, may be replicated in our edition. We do, however, repair the vast majority of imperfections successfully; any imperfections that remain are intentionally left to preserve the state of such historical works.

Forgotten Books is a registered trademark of FB &c Ltd.
Copyright © 2018 FB &c Ltd.
FB &c Ltd, Dalton House, 60 Windsor Avenue, London, SW19 2RR.
Company number 08720141. Registered in England and Wales.

For support please visit www.forgottenbooks.com

1 MONTH OF FREE READING

at
www.ForgottenBooks.com

By purchasing this book you are eligible for one month membership to ForgottenBooks.com, giving you unlimited access to our entire collection of over 1,000,000 titles via our web site and mobile apps.

To claim your free month visit:
www.forgottenbooks.com/free40582

* Offer is valid for 45 days from date of purchase. Terms and conditions apply.

English
Français
Deutsche
Italiano
Español
Português

www.forgottenbooks.com

Mythology Photography **Fiction**
Fishing Christianity **Art** Cooking
Essays Buddhism Freemasonry
Medicine **Biology** Music **Ancient Egypt** Evolution Carpentry Physics
Dance Geology **Mathematics** Fitness
Shakespeare **Folklore** Yoga Marketing
Confidence Immortality Biographies
Poetry **Psychology** Witchcraft
Electronics Chemistry History **Law**
Accounting **Philosophy** Anthropology
Alchemy Drama Quantum Mechanics
Atheism Sexual Health **Ancient History**
Entrepreneurship Languages Sport
Paleontology Needlework Islam
Metaphysics Investment Archaeology
Parenting Statistics Criminology
Motivational

he was not an old friend of Mr. Crawley's, because if he was I felt sure Mr. Crawley would be very pleased to see him; as he was a great invalid and not able to get out himself, would he please to go and see Mr. Crawley? He instantly burst out crying and said, 'Oh no, oh no!' Mr. St. John begged him to go, but he said, 'I cannot.' Mr. St. John asked him then to send his name, but he said, 'Oh no!' At last Mr. St. John said, 'You may tell Mr. Crawley Dr. Newman is here.'"

With this clue — the indomitable individuality of the man — we can follow his course without confusion, and we can understand why three of his friends at least were never fundamentally perplexed about him. When he turns to Frederick Rogers, or to R. W. Church, or to Father St. John, he always finds that they have the same confidence as ever in his intellectual and moral sincerity, and "*cor ad cor loquitur.*" To the end they manifested to him the trust and forbearance and sympathetic comprehension which it had always been Newman's dream to find in his ecclesiastical superiors, but which, whether in the Anglican or in the Roman Church, he generally failed to obtain. For these three friends of his perceived that from crisis to crisis his course throughout was like a series of the subtlest chemical reactions, in which he was fundamentally consistent with himself. Newman was always Newman. Gladstone brought this out far on in Newman's career as a Roman Catholic, when, in their discussion about Vaticanism and the Pope's Infallibility, Gladstone pushed Newman to the wall and drew from him this confession: "If I am obliged to bring religion into after-dinner toasts (which indeed does not seem quite the thing), I shall drink, — to the Pope,

LIBRARY OF THE THEOLOGICAL SEMINAR

PRINCETON, N. J.

PRESENTED BY

the Library of

the New Jersey College for Women

Division

Section

BR 1700 .D683
Douglas, George William,
  1850-1926.
Essays in appreciation

With kind regards fr
the author
George Williamson

April 1. 1913.

ESSAYS IN APPRECIATION

ESSAYS
IN APPRECIATION

BY

GEORGE WILLIAM DOUGLAS, D.D., S.T.D.

*Canon of the Cathedral of St. John the Divine,
New York*

LONGMANS, GREEN, AND CO.
FOURTH AVENUE & 30TH STREET, NEW YORK
LONDON, BOMBAY, AND CALCUTTA
1912

COPYRIGHT, 1912, BY
GEORGE WILLIAM DOUGLAS

PREFATORY NOTE

THE following notice of the Reverend Dr. Henry A. Coit was originally published in a letter to the New York *Evening Post* of February 9, 1895; that of Sister Anne Ayres was published in a sermon preached on the fifty-fourth anniversary of the Sisterhood of the Holy Communion, Feast of the Purification, February 2, 1900, in the Church of the Holy Communion, New York, at the unveiling of a memorial tablet to Sister Anne. The notices of the Reverend Dr. Morgan Dix and of the Reverend Dr. William R. Huntington were prepared for special committees appointed by Bishop Greer in behalf of the Diocese. The Minute of Bishop Potter was written for a special committee appointed by the Cathedral Chapter. The notice of the Reverend Canon Laurence Henry Schwab, D.D., was a Minute prepared for a special committee of the New York Clerical Club. The study of Cardinal Newman was published in *The Churchman* of May and June, 1912.

The article on Bishop Doane, and the review of the Revision of the Epistle to the Hebrews by Two Clerks, appeared in *The Churchman* of August 17th, 1912. The article on General Booth appeared in *The Churchman* of August 31st, 1912.

In the case of the obituary of Dr. Dix, of Dr. Huntington and of Canon Schwab, I was requested to write the testimonial in behalf of my colleagues on the committee, and their names, with mine, were signed to the same: for which reason their names are now given in a foot-note to each testimonial, by way of historical record.

Requests from various quarters have from time to time come to me for a republication of these appreciations, so that I am induced to assemble them in a less fugitive form than that in which they originally appeared. G. W. D.

CATHEDRAL OF ST. JOHN THE DIVINE,
  NEW YORK, SEPTEMBER 2, 1912.

CONTENTS

	PAGE
The Reverend Henry A. Coit	1
Sister Anne Ayres	11
The Reverend Morgan Dix	31
The Reverend William Reed Huntington	55
The Right Reverend Henry Codman Potter	69
The Reverend Canon Laurence Henry Schwab	87
Newman Once More — A Study	97
Bishop Doane — the Poet	189
An Experiment in Conservative Revision of the New Testament — A Review	197
General Booth	217

THE
REVEREND HENRY A. COIT, D.D.

THE
REVEREND HENRY A. COIT, D.D.

Rector of St. Paul's School, Concord, New Hampshire[1]

IF any man in America deserved a public funeral, it was the late rector of St. Paul's School. And yet I cannot but feel that there was something singularly appropriate in the privacy and loneliness with which, from sheer stress of weather, so far as friends from a distance were concerned, his remains were laid to rest. The three hundred school-boys on the spot must, indeed, with their teachers, have formed an imposing retinue at the burial; yet these were but a part of the vastly larger number that, under ordinary cir-

---

[1] This notice of Dr. Coit's funeral was originally published in a letter to the New York *Evening Post* of February 9, 1895.

cumstances, would have thronged about the bier. Very many of us older boys found it to be simply impossible to reach Concord in the blinding, drifting blizzard that prevailed last Friday, blocking all roads and delaying railway trains.

Nevertheless, as my mind goes back to the old days when I was a school-boy there, it seems, I say, quite in keeping with the character of our dear dead master that his burial should be thus apart and lonely, hidden by the snow. For was there ever a great man who more instinctively shrunk from publicity than Dr. Coit? Never, from start to finish, was it he that put himself forward; it was his work that thrust him into prominence. Never once, in any way, did he advertise either the school or himself. Nay, he recoiled from everything that savored of notoriety with the simple delicacy of a girl. He hated to show himself in strange places, to speak or write in them. The only place where he was thoroughly himself was at his own school, among his own boys, — there he was at home. It was his boys and under-masters, as far and wide they scattered to their homes, that advertised him; as St. Paul said of his disciples, "Ye are my epistle."

There is hardly time, as yet, to measure Dr. Coit's position among our great educators and administrators, or to tell the whole story of his distinguished career. His high position is incontestable, — so great that we can only appreciate it properly after the lapse of years, and by contrast with others who have worked in the same field. Just now, in the shock of his unexpected death, his old boys dwell naturally upon the more distinctively spiritual aspects of his character. I find recurring again and again to my memory a verse of the Psalmist: "They shall go from strength to strength, until unto the God of gods appeareth every one of them in Sion." This was one of his favorite texts. As my mind runs back to the little chapel, — the first one of the earliest days, — I recollect how that text used to crop out again and again in his sermons. I did not care much for sermons in those days, but somehow there was hardly ever a Sunday, if "the Doctor" preached, that some sentence of his did not fasten on me. Though he often repeated himself, the *connections* of his thought were so various and suggestive that I did not find the repetitions tiresome; and I well remember how surprised and interested I used to be when Sunday after Sunday this same text would once more slip into his thoughts: "They shall go from strength to strength." This was the very thing that he wanted us to do: it was what he had done himself.

Beginning with the three boys in the carriage that brought him to Dr. Shattuck's country-house, bit by bit, he had built up that great school, and had built up himself with it, — himself the stronger as his school waxed strong, — all the poetry and the sentiment of his rarely gifted nature broadening down into the fine virility of the tested man. We used to think him narrow sometimes, but I am not sure that, as we ourselves grow older, we are not coming to perceive that what we then esteemed "narrowness" was ultimate truth of insight. It is not given to many men to be thoroughly religious from the outset to the end of their lives. The heart of most men roams restlessly for a long time before it rests at last in God. But Dr. Coit was religious always. There was no humbug about him. That is why he had such power over us, in spite of ourselves. From classroom and playground to the Thursday evening talks and the daily chapel, that is the sort of a man he was, — the religious man. Here, in very truth, was a man who was "alive unto God." It seemed as if he never opened a book nor touched a topic, nor met a boy or man, without having "God in all his thoughts." And somehow he never bored us. Other men bored us boys with their religiousness, but "the Doctor" never did. Rather, it appeared as if he had merely gotten on ahead of us, and that very likely we should try to catch up with him by and by. The pathos, the beauty, the risks, the awfulness and the joy, the prospects and the power of the sincere religious life of the human soul, — they have been realized in our lifetime by this man whom we have known, whom we have called our master. It rests with us to follow, or to repudiate, the "secret of Jesus," for which he lived and died. This, I think, is the final impression which every St. Paul's boy, whether of the older time or to-day, has derived from intercourse with that great schoolmaster whose earthly remains were laid to rest last Friday, in the pure New Hampshire snows.

SISTER ANNE AYRES

SISTER ANNE AYRES [1]

ON this Feast of the Purification of the Blessed Virgin Mary, in the year of our Lord 1900, we are gathered together in this Church of the Holy Communion for a special purpose known to us beforehand. This is the anniversary of the Sisterhood of the Holy Communion, at which time it has been the custom of these Sisters to kneel together, as such, at yonder altar, and partake of the Body and Blood of Jesus Christ our Lord; but on this occasion we are invited to fix our thoughts on the life and work of one particular woman, a tablet to whose memory is here unveiled

---

[1] This notice was the concluding portion of the sermon preached on the fifty-fourth anniversary of the Sisterhood of the Holy Communion, Feast of the Purification, February 2, 1900, in the Church of the Holy Communion, New York, at the unveiling of a memorial tablet to Sister Anne Ayres.

to-day. The Sisterhood of the Holy Communion was founded, under God, by Anne Ayres, at the suggestion of William Augustus Muhlenberg. Like all things of deep spiritual import, neither he who, under God, made the suggestion, nor she in whose soul the suggestion lodged, perceived beforehand what the outcome of it would be. According to our Saviour's parable, there was "first the blade, then the ear, after that the full corn in the ear." In the summer of 1845, there was gathered on Sunday in the little chapel of St. Paul's College, a small congregation, among whom, the record declares, were Dr. Muhlenberg's sister, his niece, and some friends who were spending their vacation at College Point, Long Island; and when to these Dr. Muhlenberg preached a sermon on "Jephtha's Vow," with an application glancing at the blessedness of giving one's self undividedly to God's service,[1] neither he nor his audience guessed that his covert and guarded suggestion would ultimately bear fruit in the Sisterhood of the Holy Communion; yet Anne Ayres, who was one of that little congregation, lived to testify that then and thereby she was inspired to take the successive steps which, seven years afterwards, in a different place and very different circumstances, resulted in the formation of the Sisterhood of the Holy Communion.

I do not propose to attempt to-day a biography of Sister Anne Ayres, nor to dwell on the three main stages of her work for Christ and his Church: first, in this parish of the Holy Communion, which gave the name to the sisterhood which

---

[1] See "Life and Work of Dr. Muhlenberg," by Anne Ayres, p. 189: New York, Thomas Whittaker.

she founded; second, in St. Luke's Hospital; and last of all, in St. Johnland. I hardly think that she, from her place in Paradise, would care to have me emphasize, before God's altar, the days of the years of her earthly pilgrimage, nor the temporal and temporary aspects of her labor, even though the monuments thereof be as notable as these. Rather she would have us express our thoughts of her this morning in the words of the familiar saint's day hymn:

"From all Thy saints in warfare, for all Thy saints at rest,
To Thee, O blessed Jesus, all praises be addressed.
Thou, Lord, didst win the battle, that they might conquerors be;
Their crowns of living glory are lit with rays from Thee."

And so, instead of dwelling on the details of her earthly service of our Master and Saviour, I desire to bring out, if I can, the salient motive, the inner spiritual ideal which actuated her, and which rendered her service, in a sense, peculiar. For at the epoch when her lifework began, the duty which she undertook was, in a true sense, peculiar, so far at least as our Anglican Communion was concerned. It was laid upon Anne Ayres to revive in the Protestant Episcopal Church of the United States of America the ancient Catholic idea of woman's undivided service for Christ and His Church, whether in connection with the administration of divine worship in God's house, or of works of mercy, or of Christian education. If you will read her biography of Dr. Muhlenberg with close attention from end to end, you will finally perceive what the underlying idea of her own life was, and what were the range and the atmosphere in which her spirit moved; or if you are still in some doubt about it, your doubts will be dispelled when you peruse, in the volume entitled "Evangelical Catholic Papers," which Anne Ayres also edited, Dr. Muhlenberg's essay on "Protestant Sisterhoods."

In the history of the long, large life of the Church Catholic as a whole, the work of women specially set apart for Christ's service has assumed, in the main, one or other of three forms: First there is the work of the deaconess proper, which is, in its main idea, individual and single; even as that of each of the three orders of the Christian ministry proper, bishops, priests, and deacons, is, in its main idea, individual and single; and the deaconess is intended to be the workfellow and assistant of some particular bishop, or, under the bishop, of some parish priest or rector. Secondly, there is the corporate sisterhood, whereby a number of women, each of whom is for her own part consecrated individually to work for Christ and His Church, go further and band themselves together in an Order, where there is careful, corporate discipline, with a head and members, and a central home, and a visible property, and an organized rule partaking of the military. Here the connection with some parish priest or rector, and the obedience to some bishop, is less complete and continuous; the idea of the order is paramount, and each order of sisters is likely, in process of time, to acquire an entity and traditions of its own. Thirdly, besides these two — the single deaconess on the one hand, and the corporate sisterhood on the other — the vocation of women set apart to Christian work in the Church has taken a form which partakes of the characteristics of both of the others and is intermediary between them. Of this third type of the service of women in the Church the Kaiserswerth Deaconess Association, as established by the Lutheran Pastor Fliedner, affords the best known example; although lately in the Church of England, associations of women have arisen, calling themselves sometimes deaconesses, sometimes sisters, which seem to be successful instances of the same general method. In this third type, while the idea of the corporation is kept in the background, subordinate to that of the deaconess or sister as an individual servant of the Church for Christ's sake, nevertheless there is a recognized community, to which the individual belongs for a longer or shorter period; and this community life entails the undoubted advantages of mutual sympathy and support, and greater unity and efficiency in action; the various individuals with various gifts being held together under an acknowledged leader of their own kind and sex, so long as they choose to remain together. Each of these three main forms of woman's work in the Church has its evident advantages, and each also its drawbacks and dangers. And underlying each and all of them is this main question to be settled: whether the woman's dedication to her work shall be for a period of time, at her own discretion, or for life under a vow. Among Roman Catholics some of the strictest conventual orders take vows for definite periods, renewable from time to time; and even where the vow is meant to be for life, it is nevertheless in the power of the Pope or bishop to give release. And, on the other hand, in the case of the Protestant Deaconess Association at Kaiserswerth, and of those associations in our Anglican Communion which resemble it, although the vows are in form renewable from time to time, nevertheless the spirit, and the practical ideals of the association, as now developed and crystallized, are such that the individual members, even though they be Lutherans, distinctly lose caste, and are considered by their associates to have fallen from their true profession, if they give up the regular deaconess work and marry, or go back into the secular world. Now, as far as our own Anglican Communion is concerned, no one who is familiar with the history of the last sixty years can fail to perceive that all these three types of women-workers for Christ and His Church have made themselves at home among us. When Sister Anne Ayres was first set apart by Dr. Muhlenberg one winter evening in this church where we are now gathered, after daily service was over and the congregation dispersed, and only the priest and the postulant were left, she on her knees before the chancel rail and he in his surplice within, with the good old sexton as the only witness, waiting to put out the lights — when, I say, Sister Anne Ayres was thus set apart, she evidently had in mind to found an organized body of sisters not unlike the Kaiserswerth deaconesses. And such, on the whole and in a general way, was the character of the association which she did inaugurate, and which, changing somewhat with the changing years, exists to-day under the name of the Sisterhood of the Holy Communion. Ere long, three of those who were at first associated thus, desiring a stricter, closer, and more formal organization, left the Sisterhood of the Holy Communion and founded the

Sisterhood of St. Mary, whose noble work has likewise been widely recognized and blest throughout our Church in this country and beyond it. Meanwhile, Sister Anne Ayres followed Dr. Muhlenberg himself first to St. Luke's Hospital and afterward to St. Johnland; and, though she still worked more or less as one of the Sisters of the Holy Communion, nevertheless, by reason of her practical independence, she in effect reverted in later years to what New Testament scholars regard as probably the most primitive of all the types of woman's formal ministry in the Christian Church, namely, the single deaconess, like Phœbe commended of St. Paul. Anne Ayres was not called by this name of deaconess, for she was still known as Sister Anne, and was often side by side with her old associates; nevertheless, her actual work, in its comparative separateness and singleness, its dependence on the single pastor alone, and in other regards easily distinguishable — her actual work was rather like that which is now conducted under our recent Canon of Deaconesses. And in this Anne Ayres was following not merely the leading of circumstances, but the final bent of Dr. Muhlenberg's mind, and doubtless of her own.

Whatever their original intention may have been in 1845, the ultimate feeling as to the work they wished to prosecute is clearly expressed in Dr. Muhlenberg's paper on "Protestant Sisterhoods," which was issued in 1852:

"When the Sisterhood degenerates it will come to an end. It depends for its continuance wholly upon the continuance of the zeal which called it into being. The uniting principle among its members is their common affection for the object which has brought them together; but there is no constraint from without on the part of the Church, nor any from within, in the form of religious vows or promises to one another, to insure their freedom of conscience as individuals. Not that they hold themselves ever ready to adjourn. Each and all feel that they have entered upon a sacred service, which they are at liberty to quit only at the demand of duty elsewhere. Handmaidens of the Lord, waiting upon his good pleasure, they are not anxious for the future, content to leave it in His hands. We want no combinations, no widespread order of charity, under one head or Church control, nor in any way capable of holding property in their own right."

Such was Sister Anne's view of her vocation; and it was in strict keeping with the above quoted sentiments that when the course of years, duty, as she believed, called her less and less to associate work, and more and more to individual work, she lived more as a single worker. Far be it from you or me, my brethren, to say that one of these types of workers that I have mentioned is better or more useful than the others. Human nature has many sides, and opportunities for Church work vary in their aspects and demands. The wind of God, the Holy Spirit that moves individual souls to this task or to that, bloweth where it listeth; and thou hearest the sound thereof, but canst not tell whence it cometh or whither it goeth. Our Church in these last fifty years has found a place and function for each of these methods of work; and noble and notable results have been accomplished by all these types of laborers in the vineyard. Some women are called of God to one of these vocations, some to another; and, under certain safeguards which history and experience suggest, all of these ministries are likely to be wanted in the future, as they have been in the past. Each type has its strong points and its weak points, its peculiar disabilities and limitations, and each its own reward — the "name that no man knoweth, save he that receiveth it."

But my duty to-day is a simple one: to single out and emphasize the particular type of character and of task which belonged to this woman whose noble name we distinguish for commemoration, and the tablet to whose memory we to-day unveil. And what I desire to say in conclusion is this: I chose my text because it suggested, as I believe, the key-note of the character of Sister Anne Ayres. Just in proportion as our work for Christ is a separate and single work, not supported by definite and indissoluble ties to some large organization, just in that proportion, if we are to succeed and to persevere, do we need to realize what our text expresses — the absolute nearness of God to the soul, and the absolute dependence of each single soul on God. "All live unto Him." "My soul hangeth on Thee." Here is where the really devout Romanist and the really devout Protestant meet on common ground — John Bunyan, and John Wesley, and John Keble, with Xavier and Loyola and François de Sales and Fénelon. You may criticise these men, for they were human; you may differ from them, for they were fallible; but you cannot deny that, one and all, they were permeated through and through by the consciousness of God our Father; that day by day and hour by hour they "looked to Him." And such, too, was Anne Ayres. This it was which enabled her to be true to her vocation up to the very end without resting on those outward helps of association and daily rule which most of us require to keep us straight and true. It seemed as if she never met a human being, without first saying secretly to herself that ejaculation of the saint: "In whatsoever way Thou willest, bind me faster to Thee." In her was manifested the power of the personal recollection of God to reinforce and fructify the other powers of mankind; and there lay the secret of her pervasive influence over her fellows. Other people might tell them, but she first made them feel that for each and all of us there is but one life to live, and that directly with God. "As the eyes of a maiden unto the hand of her mistress, so her eyes looked unto the Lord her God."

THE REVEREND MORGAN DIX

THE REVEREND MORGAN DIX

ON Saturday, May 2, A.D. 1908, at a meeting of the Clergy who were present at the funeral of the Rev'd Morgan Dix, S.T.D., LL.D., D.C.L., late Rector of Trinity Church, New York, the undersigned were appointed by the Rt. Rev'd David H. Greer, D.D., Bishop Coadjutor of the Diocese, as a Committee to draft resolutions or a Minute, expressive of the feelings of those present and of those unavoidably absent, in view of our recent bereavement.[1] What we say can but imperfectly convey an idea of the depth of the impression made

---

[1] The names of the Committee were:
>WILLIAM T. MANNING,
>WILLIAM R. HUNTINGTON,
>J. LEWIS PARKS,
>GEORGE WILLIAM DOUGLAS,
>WILLIAM M. GROSVENOR.

by the sudden departure of this distinguished man, who was also to many of us brother, pastor, and friend. Events of this importance call forth more than the grief naturally caused by the visit of death to the house: they shock men by the consciousness that a treasure jointly owned by large numbers has been taken from their hands, and that a force potent for good throughout the community has been withdrawn to a higher sphere. He whom we have lost may be said to have belonged to the whole Church, and to the people at large; he was a link whereby men of divers names and vocations and origin were united, in one way or another, in the great household of God which is larger than any parish, or city, or diocese, and even than any nation.

We think of him first as a representative of the Diocese of New York in the

General Convention of our American Church, where for years he presided in the House of Deputies with rare dignity, courtesy, and justice; and with that characteristic intellectual poise and spiritual detachment which commanded the confidence and regard of his associates. Although in matters ecclesiastical he was a man of strong personal convictions evident to all, no one could accuse him of unfair partisanship in the presidential chair, and political wire-pulling was to him impossible. Even when gainsaying an antagonist, his opposition did not leave a sting, — so much so, that in his later years many of his theological opponents, in our Communion and in other Communions, struck hands with him in a feeling of true fellowship, having learned from him a lesson of agreement in controversy, and of tolerant devotion to the common cause which it is never too late to learn. As a debater in the Convention his speech was always weighty; for his thought was clear and his words were few, though charged, when necessary, with a fire that was none the less effective because it was kept down. And these same traits had long previously manifested themselves in the councils and committees of the Diocese of New York, and in all the various organizations, educational, civic, and eleëmosynary, of which he was a member. To many of these as Rector of Trinity Church he belonged *ex officio;* but he brought to them not merely the prestige of his great position, but the influence of his high personal character, of his regularity and faithfulness.

We think of him next as Rector of the mother church of New York, the most important parish in this country, whose wealth, inherited from earlier days and a different national régime, has rendered the corporation of "The Rector, Wardens, and Vestrymen of Trinity Church, New York," the most potent parochial organization, for good or evil, in the world. When Morgan Dix became its Rector two generations ago, although this parish was even then relatively a power in the land, it was, from the standpoint of our time, "the day of small things." Dr. Dix came to it in the truest sense a citizen to the manner born; representing the best results so far of the social, academic, and professional culture of this community. With the exception of less than three years, he had lived his life and done his work as a school-boy, as a collegian, as a seminarian, and as an ecclesiastic, in the city of New York; whereas among his most noted contemporaries few were city born. It is proverbial that the sons of rich men and of great men seldom enhance the station which they inherit; but Dr. Dix added ten talents to his inherited ten, and that in full view of the community which held in recollection his father's record of civic and personal distinction. In the words of the Psalmist, "God heard his vows, and gave him the heritage of those that fear God's name." The faith which dwelt first in his father and his mother was in him also, — a blessed predestination to the life of faith, to which he was not disobedient in the patient, laborious years of a long career. To the end his early home explained him; yet he outgrew it as a strong man should, growing from strength to strength; although the sweet memories of it, and the sense of the everlasting value of the home, clung to him. As a boy he knew the joys of social refinement and ample means, the wit and wisdom of the intellectual life fraught with historic associations. He had behind him a strong mother and a patriotic father who, between them, created an atmosphere for their son, wherein the quality of the scholar and the artist blended with something of the soldier who feared God but not man, and understood that duty is stern. His father was a public man, and it was an industrious home, with the same habits of quiet punctuality which were afterward to characterize the Rector of Trinity Parish throughout his life. Fond of frolic with his intimates, and possessed of abounding humor to oil the wheels of labor, young Dix seemed nevertheless from the start to be enlisted like a soldier to accept as a matter of course the tasks of a vast routine. For little things and great things he was alike conscientiously responsible, and wonderful for equanimity and quiet nerves.

Upon the Christian Ministry he entered with evident awe, and a certain consequent severity is visible in the portrait of him by Huntington, painted after the full rectorship of Trinity Parish had been laid upon his shoulders. From that day forward his influence radiated from the posts whence the true priest's influence always radiates: the altar and the pulpit. Whatever Morgan Dix was elsewhere began from what he was in the pulpit and at the altar. No breath of scandalous suspicion, no attribution of wrong motives ever tarnished his name. He bore the message, and he had the mind of Christ. Over in England, in those days — the days that followed the Tractarian Movement — it was said of Oxford that the most remarkable thing about it was not the architecture and traditions, but the number of men you met in the streets and quadrangles whom you knew to be unworldly, "setting their affections on things above, not on things on the earth"; and such was the inevitable impression that Dr. Dix made on all who knew him. A lady who at that period met him, unobserved, as he was walking his accustomed way to his office of a weekday, said of him, "Ah, you can see in his face that he is determined to keep the devil down." He had a profound sense of the supernatural. And to this was added the inimitable impression of intellectual and moral certainty, of religious conviction. "He knew Whom he had believed." While many of his contemporaries were shifting their theological positions from time to time under the stress of new influences, early in his ministry he took his position promptly, and kept it thereafter on the whole. Standing on what he felt was a theological *terra firma*, he did his best work and dealt his best blows at an age when most clergymen are beating the air; and always his predominating zeal was for the glory of God and the salvation of souls. His real work in those days was his cure of souls, in which he developed an intense spiritual energy; and, besides this, to vindicate for our American Church her title-deeds as a child of the mother Church of England, and thereby her title to the inheritance, the spirit, and the aims and obligations of the Church Catholic and Apostolic, wherein we affirm our belief in the Creeds. To Dr. Dix's mind the *Via Media* of the Oxford Tractarians was not a theory, but a fact, preserved in our Prayer Book and realized among us. He was sure that the Anglican Church went into the crucible of the Reformation as the Church of England, and came out of it as the Church of England, and planted afterward in America this Church of ours as a true daughter of the ancient stock. Therefore when he spoke of the Catholic Church and churchmen of earlier ages — of a Leo, or a Gregory, or an Augustine, or a Chrysostom — it was as of his own forbears in the ministry of Christ to men. His mind was attuned to Holy Scripture as expounded by the early Fathers, and their prayers and the early Liturgies fell naturally from his lips, — so naturally, that there was no book of private devotions which he preferred to Bishop Andrewes's in the original Greek and Latin, where the expressions of the

Scriptures and the Fathers and the Liturgies are fused in one. Withal he had an innate sense of law. He never practised any ritual which he did not believe to be lawful in this land and Church of ours, and his supreme care was for the beauty of holiness. No one could doubt that who ever heard him pray. By the bedside of the sick he might at first sight be esteemed somewhat cold and reserved, a trifle constrained in manner; but when he fell upon his knees all that passed away, and there came into his voice in prayer a beseeching, penetrating tone which, once heard, could never be forgotten. Then you knew that Dr. Dix watched for souls, as they that must give account. And, unlike many clergymen, he was able to carry this same beseeching, penetrating tone into his rendering of the public prayers, so that his intoning of the

Church Service was a model in its easy naturalness and sweetness. He did not "sing," he "said" the prayers, in the true sense of the old Prayer Book rubric. And the rare recollection of mind and concentration of spirit with which he celebrated Holy Communion made one feel as if so it must have been said in the Catacombs by the martyrs, ere they went forth to the lions. When he entered the pulpit there was something of the same. Bishop Hobart in the pulpit of Trinity Church had rendered the former style of conventional eloquence impossible; and when Dr. Dix followed him, after an interval, through all the pulpits of the parish the knell of the old embroidered sermon was sounded. Alike in the chapels and the mother church the effect was noticeable on all his assistants of the terse, incisive beauty of the Rector's style and his English undefiled. No man in America could make words serve him with finer skill than Morgan Dix, and to those who knew the English tongue and literature his sentences were packed with subtle allusions and references that were a constant charm even on the printed page; but when he spoke from the pulpit there was, when he was at his best, the added power of a voice that could be resonant and sharp with reprobation, or full of melody and tenderest appeal. Withal he possessed the power of the true judge's charge to the jury; his statement of the case was the best of arguments.

It is impossible in this Minute to tell the story of his multiform activities, or even to allude to all of them, or to the books he published. We have dwelt rather on his more personal traits of character, for another generation will know nothing of these; but we have known them, and now we feel their loss. Mention must at least be made of his work in promoting the organization of the Sisters of St. Mary, whose director he was for years, and for whom he composed the Book of Hours, which of its kind is a landmark in this country, and indicates the range and accuracy of Dr. Dix's liturgical knowledge and taste. Dr. Muhlenberg had led the way, and had developed the idea of Sisterhoods up to a certain point; but it was chiefly Dr. Dix, with the sanction of Bishop Horatio Potter and the weight of Trinity Church, who really secured for Sisters, in the conventual sense of the term, a place and a hearing in our American Church. For scholarship proper he had little time, though the disposition and tools of the scholar were amply his; and in his earlier ministry his published commentaries on St. Paul's Epistles to the Romans, Galatians, and Colossians gave testimony to his bent. He was often in those days the object of scurrilous abuse, and was accused of Romanizing; whereas in fact he gave to Tractarianism a steady base in America, and proved once more the truth of the observation that few who studied the Scriptures deeply have gone over from our Communion to the Church of Rome. For the improvement of Church Music, and the progress among us of the Choral Service, he did more than will ever be known; for into this, in his unobtrusive way, he threw the whole influence and the resources of his parish; and somehow many clergymen and laymen, who would not have liked such music or such methods for themselves, seemed to feel that it was well and proper for Trinity Parish to show what might be done in that line if anybody had the means and a mind to.

When he came to his parish in 1862, besides Trinity Church there were only St. Paul's and St. John's and Trinity Chapel; with their Churchyards which, when there was a move to sell them as valuable real estate, his ardent sense of the Christian's duty to the dead enabled him to have preserved as silent witnesses, amidst this world's business, to our faith in the life of the world to come. But although Dr. Dix's administration was thus conservative, he was keen to perceive that the main task of a rich church should be among the poor. Not only did he, as Assistant Rector, reside in a house in Hubert Street among the poor; not only did he, as Rector, insist for many years on living in the old Varick Street Rectory long after that neighborhood had been deserted by the fashionable; not only did he find his greatest happiness in his day-school and Sunday-school and house-to-house visiting among the poor; but during his rectorship it began to be his vestry's policy to establish new mission chapels, besides Trinity Chapel and St. Agnes' which ministered rather to the well-to-do. Hence arose St. Chrysostom's and St. Augustine's Chapels; and St. Cornelius' for the soldiers on Governor's Island; while All Saints', Henry Street, and St. Luke's, Hudson Street, and finally the Church of the Intercession far uptown, were one by one taken under Trinity's fostering care. Meanwhile the chancel of Trinity Church was enlarged and beautified by the Astor-memorial reredos; St Paul's and St. John's Chapels were renovated and embellished; and the old Rectory in Varick Street was transformed into a Hospital, as the condition on which the Rector would consent to move up-town to the new Rectory adjacent to Trinity Chapel. Dr. Dix's personal gifts to charitable objects were unstinted, but little published: his own left hand hardly knew what his right hand did. Furthermore, in the progress of the years, much of what is now known as the Settlement idea of parish work was anticipated in Trinity Mission House and the operations of the Trinity Church Association. These works do follow him. Now that he has been withdrawn from us, by these his monuments shall we renew our memories of him with respect and admiration and the tender regard that belong to one who was faithful in the opportunities of a manifold career, calm under frequent misunderstandings and misrepresentations, courageous in adversity, and most beloved by those who knew him best.

The home circle is sacred: we may not there intrude. But it is a matter of common knowledge that all children took to him instinctively, and he loved their ways, full of the spirit of Alice in Wonderland. By his talents for drawing with pen and pencil, and of musical improvisation, he was able to engage the fancy of all childlike spirits, young or old. With his wife and children we sympathize in their sorrow, praying that both they and we, with him who has gone before to Paradise, may be found at last in Christ, heirs together of the grace of life.

Brethren, the time is short. The lines which Copernicus traced for his own tombstone were a favorite prayer of Dr. Dix's, and they furnish for ourselves a fitting close to this insufficient sketch of the great and noble soul, our brother in the Ministry, who has gone to his last account:

> Non parem Pauli gratiam requiro,
> Veniam Petri neque posco, sed quam
> In Crucis ligno dederas latroni
>   Sedulus oro.

THE REVEREND WILLIAM REED HUNTINGTON, D.D., D.C.L., L.H.D.

THE REVEREND WILLIAM REED HUNTINGTON, D.D., D.C.L., L.H.D.[1]

THE undersigned,[1] a Committee appointed by the Bishop of New York to draft a Minute on the death of the Rev. William Reed Huntington, D.D., D.C.L., L.H.D., late rector of Grace Church, New York, cannot find words to express the thoughts and feelings which crowd for utterance. To his mourning family we offer our heartfelt sympathy; and there is a general sense of emptiness, not only in the diocese of New York, but in our whole American

---

[1] Obituary Minute adopted by the Committee of Clergymen appointed by the Bishop of New York. The names of the Committee were:
>GEORGE WILLIAM DOUGLAS,
>WILLIAM T. MANNING,
>J. LEWIS PARKS,
>ERNEST M. STIRES,
>CORNELIUS B. SMITH.

Church, now that this great man is gone. For his was a personality singularly exuberant in natural gifts of intellect and spirit; moreover, the grace of God abounded in him. He was great as a seer and prophet; as an organizer and administrator; as an ecclesiastical statesman; as a master of the English tongue, thinking incisively and speaking winged words, most powerful in parliamentary debate; as a pastor of troubled souls; as a friend of his fellows, faithful to the uttermost. He never shirked a burden which belonged to him, and he shared unselfishly the burdens of many others. His long career was marked by rare consistency: one always knew where to find him. Keenly alive to the weaknesses of men and the evils of the day, he was nevertheless no pessimist; rather he was persistently hopeful of men and things, and at three-score and ten he was still ready for vast enterprises, manifesting in manifold activities his unique resourcefulness.

In social intercourse his humor and alert intellectuality were sweetened by the gentleness of spirit which was never quite hidden beneath his mantle of natural reserve. He did not ask for sympathy, but was quick to extend it to all who opened to him a truly troubled heart. Sincere himself to the very core, he elicited sincerity from every one with whom he had to do; and many who had felt in him something of the shrewd Puritan, bred in the nipping and the eager air of Eastern Massachusetts, found in Dr. Huntington, when sorrow fell upon them, a pastor of souls whose touch was like an angel of mercy.

He would not wish us to dwell here on

the achievements of his life, so uncommonly successful, so thorough in its service. But at least mention must be made of his work in the General Convention for the enrichment of the Prayer Book, and for its more flexible use; of his lifelong zeal for Church unity; of his splendid part in the upbuilding of the New York cathedral; and of the exhibition, in and through his great parish, of what the "Institutional Church" might be when the proper man and the proper circumstances meet, and there is the strength of will not to let worship be overborne by clubs and classes.

It was a characteristic act of his when, at the period of life fixed in his mind beforehand, he tendered his resignation as rector of Grace Church. In his own lion-heart he did not feel superannuated; but if his Vestry thought that his day was done, he was willing to retire. And when they signified their unwillingness to let him go, with the gladsome energy of interior conviction he buckled on his harness once again. Equally characteristic was his use of the fund which, at this juncture, was raised for him as a personal testimonial from admiring parishioners. A stranger to the situation and the man might have deemed it ungracious on his part to decline to use the income of that fund for himself, so long as he was able to continue at his post; but his friends recognized that it was simply the sternly conscientious Christian man — with a touch of the old Puritan in him coming out once more in the sweet guise of self-denial — refusing to divert to his personal comfort, even if deserved, the largess of his people, which, in his judgment, would be better devoted to God's poor.

That one act of his, in its rigid charitableness, wrought more for the cause of Christ in this community than many larger bounties more widely advertised.

In any account of him one trait cannot be passed over: his instinctive faculty for leading men. Real leadership is rare. Most men, it has been remarked, enjoy the luxury of being commandeered in thought and action. But every now and then a man appears who is born to lead. The man himself could not tell how he does it. He simply *is*. And somehow, even if his associates at times mistrust his judgment, they find positive delight in following him notwithstanding. Who lives shall see the end of the matter; but this man feels sure beforehand, and never quails. He does not accomplish his effects by ingenuity or subtlety, or by the arts of petty diplomacy; but in broad, sudden ways he does what he wants and says what he means, and chooses from his followers the right man for the right place, and goes ahead. You may not say that he possesses this or that single quality conspicuously; you may rather say that of some of those who co-operate with him as his deputies. But although the deputies may even seem to surpass the master in separate qualities of brain or of morale, nevertheless he dominates and guides, and in his presence dissent is seldom audible. Not that he has an overweening and disagreeable ambition to impress himself, but there is an aura of personality about the master which silences opposition and secures compliance and fealty. This is sometimes so even if the leader be not a supremely good man; but when genuine goodness is superadded to the rest, then the effect is beyond compare.

And such was Dr. Huntington. What rendered him, as a leader, most difficult to withstand, was his intrepid righteousness. Those who opposed him were obliged to feel that their own desires must be purged of much dross before they could compete with his. His strength was as the strength of ten, because his heart was pure. It was his uncommon personal integrity, his entire truthfulness, that fused in him what to many seemed to be the contradictory tendencies of his temperament, radical and conservative. On the one hand, he could not bear that men of the present should halt and stumble over the rubbish of the past; and this made him radical in the eyes of some. On the other hand, he had too keen a sense of the continuity and vital force of human history, and of ecclesiastical institutions, to be willing to break rashly with real traditions; so that he often surprised by his conservatism people who expected him to be radical. Yet both radicals and conservatives, when they were personally thrown with this great leader, ended by applying to him the saying of the prophet Micah: "He hath shewed thee, O man, what is good."

He saw men and things always in the mirror of eternity, and therefore he was a man of prayer. From the pulpit of Grace Church he made his hearers feel that they were set apart awhile from the flowing of time, and were dealing with the life that shall always be. We must find our minimum of faith not outside of us, but in us; not in the old learning or experience of others, nor in any science outside of us to-day, but within the heart of whatever science or experience we have made or own. He would shake religion from its wrappings for us.

New York will be a different place without him. We want these public souls — men who, as Carlyle says, know God otherwise than by hearsay, and can tell us what divine work is actually to be done here and now in the streets of New York, and not of a different work which behooved to be done in old Judea — men of whom no infidel would ever think what Voltaire is reported to have said of the preacher Massillon: "It is in vain you try to preach to me, for you are not really my enemy." Dr. Huntington, like the rest of us, was overwhelmed by the awful mystery of life and death, of past and present and the world to come; yet in it all there was for him but one controlling question: What is the mind of Christ about it? and what the great, unresting, merciful Heart of the Universe? Dr.

Huntington was sure that Jesus knows: that whoso hath seen Him hath seen the Father; and that by His life we have the light of the knowledge of the glory of God in the face of Jesus Christ. Therefore with the absorption of a tireless, effective man, as a disciple of Jesus, loving the work more than the rewards, he went about doing good; and his works do follow him. He might have been a bishop; but he preferred to lead from lower down; and from his metropolitan parish his influence penetrated to the corners of our commonwealth, and far beyond. His vision was so vast of the possibilities of religion in our time that he could not but be unselfish: he would not keep for himself what was meant for mankind. For him human life, in Church and out of Church, is a perpetual education in living with God and loving God; and to be alive to beautiful things and do heroic deeds — to smile and suffer and forbear; to choose what is hard rather than what is easy, and what is pure rather than impure, here on earth for a little while — is to perform the first act of that everlasting drama which is eternal life with God. So, as he spoke to us and acted in our midst, we could see the *gaudia certaminis* in his face; as when, in Tennyson's allegory of the Round Table, Sir Galahad answers to the protests of his king, who would withhold him from his arduous quest:

> "But I, Sir Arthur, saw the Holy Grail.
> I saw the Holy Grail, and heard a cry —
> O Galahad, and O Galahad, follow me."

THE RIGHT REVEREND HENRY CODMAN POTTER
SEVENTH BISHOP OF NEW YORK

THE RIGHT REVEREND HENRY CODMAN POTTER

On Tuesday, September 15, 1908, at a regular quarterly meeting of the Chapter of the Cathedral of St. John the Divine, New York, the undersigned [1] were appointed a Committee to draft a Minute expressive of the Chapter's feelings in view of the death of our Bishop, the Rt. Rev. Henry Codman Potter, D.D., LL.D., D.C.L., at Cooperstown, N.Y., on Tuesday, July 21.

The shock of his death came to the members of our Chapter at a season when we were widely scattered, yet the lapse of time has but made us more conscious of

---

[1] The names of the Committee were:
GEORGE F. NELSON,
GEORGE WILLIAM DOUGLAS,
ERNEST VOORHIS.

the difficulty of giving adequate expression to the sentiments that fill our hearts. For Bishop Potter was no ordinary man — no ordinary ecclesiastic. He was cast in a large mould, with a robust personality distinctly his own; as has been amply declared by the numerous letters and testimonials, from home and abroad, which have been published concerning him. It is not the duty of this Cathedral Chapter to attempt to trace the outlines of his long, laborious, and successful life, whether as pastor, as preacher, as secretary of the House of Bishops, as assistant bishop, or as the ecclesiastical head of this most important and difficult diocese, which requires a greater variety of episcopal abilities than any other in our American Church. Beginning his career in the counting-house of a mercantile concern in Philadelphia, early in life he turned of his own accord to the calling of a Christian minister; for which, beside the preparation of his distinguished parentage, he had, as the sequel showed, a distinct vocation of his own from Jesus Christ, the Shepherd and Bishop of our souls. And on everything that he touched from youth to old age he left his mark. Endowed with rare social gifts, aristocratic in his tastes and of cultured breeding, he was heartily democratic in his sympathies, with a strong sense of civic duty guided and controlled by his consciousness of responsibility as an ambassador of Christ. As shown by his Yale Lectures on "The Citizen in his Relation to the Industrial Situation," he despised the spirit of social caste; and the ideal of social brotherhood aroused his energies to practical effect throughout his ministry. To his mind, this was a part of his prophetic function. Although, as has been well said of him, he loved to be alone with his Bible and Prayer Book, brooding over life's mysteries and problems; although, wise man that he was, he was reticent of much that his large heart and fair mind knew of the backwaters and eddies of human enterprise and morality; although he denied himself many an opportunity to tell all that he believed to be true, and much that was dear to him,— nevertheless in times of political emergency, national or local, and in moments of social derangement, he was never silent when speech from him was really called for, and he had an intense sense of social compunction. All through his life laymen who were in close companionship with him set singular value on his friendship and felt the spell of his personal charm; and there are obscure country homes and rectories where his visits were an event, as the coming of one who, though he was a citizen of the great world of which they saw little, yet found their simple firesides so truly interesting that they miss him now. He always aimed to get so in touch with every man, and with every party of men, that they might be sure of his sympathy as their father in God, who entered into their life. He never tried to hide the breadth and vigor of his natural tastes, his simple enjoyment of God's world; but all men could see that he held himself in the leash of self-denial, wearing the yoke of Christ. It was felt that he really sought to use this world, as not abusing it; for the fashion of this world passeth away. Masterful by natural disposition, and possessed during his manifold career of many opportunities of mastery, he tried faithfully to rule by love, and by the power of good judgment and the patient expectation of good will on the part of those with whom he had to do. With the statesman's genius for perceiving the time-spirit — the momentary reactions and tendencies of men and things which no mere man can stem — he would quickly take the lead when he saw opportunities of civic usefulness for those who call themselves Christians; with the result that the Bishop of New York became, during his episcopate, a more potent factor than ever before in this community of vast organizations and strong individualities. In him the personality promoted the office, and the office sanctioned the personality. Beside the influence of his charm and impressiveness in personal intercourse, he was an accomplished speaker in the pulpit and on the platform, uniting ease with earnestness, grace with dignity, a lambent wit with unfeigned sympathy. Hence among all who came within his range there is a feeling that a noble figure has vanished from our midst.

And in matters more strictly ecclesiastical, after twenty-five years of comparative concord in his diocese, by virtue of his fair-mindedness, he might truly have made his own the remark of the late Bishop Wilberforce of Oxford, England: "I should scorn to be the bishop of a party, because I am a bishop of the Church of Christ." In a very real, though different, sense Bishop Potter did for his diocese what John Henry Newman, in his farewell sermon to his congregation at Littlemore, hinted that he had done for them; he interpreted his diocese to itself; reflected and made vivid and energetic the disposition and desires and views of the people committed to his care: "read their wants and feelings to them, and comforted them by the very reading."

Such were the qualities that rendered Bishop Henry Codman Potter impressive in this cathedral; which, by the coincidence of time, will be his monument, since it came into visible being during his episcopate, and here his body shall be entombed. In view of his fine appreciation of the beautiful and the imposing, it is fitting that his monument should be a feature of what he hoped would be a great and solemnizing temple to God Most High. According to its constitution, this cathedral is intended to be a house of God for all people, and it was indeed to all the people that our Bishop addressed himself. He desired the cathedral to be a consecrated acknowledgment of human relationship in the presence of the Heavenly

Father, and under the sign of the Cross. After returning from Europe several years ago, speaking of the scheme for cathedral work and maintenance, the Bishop said: "I am confirmed in my opinion that our plans regarding the new cathedral which our Church is building in this city are wise. I refer to the endowment feature. I attended service in St. Paul's Cathedral, in London, only a few Sundays ago, and I witnessed a most impressive spectacle — eight thousand people gathered under the great dome to worship. There was the 'cabby' in his fustian jacket, the porter and the railroad man, rubbing elbows with the aristocracy of Great Britain. That is essentially the cathedral idea."

Indeed, in the Bishop's ideas for the cathedral that same underlying feeling for the people and about the people was ever present, which, in a different connection, he expressed so beautifully in his memorable address on the occasion of the unveiling of the monument to the soldier dead of New York on the field of Gettysburg. "There is," he said, "no greatness in the people equal to a great vision in an emergency, and with a great courage with which to seize it. And that, I maintain, was the supreme glory of the heroes whom we commemorate to-day. Do you tell me that they were unknown, that they commanded no battalions, determined no policies, sat in no military councils, rode at the head of no regiments? Be it so! All the more are they the fitting representatives of you and me — the people."

It was with such feelings for the people that our Bishop went on with the building of this cathedral, and gathered about him the Cathedral Chapter. He wanted his cathedral church to help the Church generally to rise above the mere parochial spirit of a previous generation, and, like St. Paul, "to be all things to all men, that we may by all means save some." He wanted us to be deeply interested in the sociological field of the Church; to study the causes and the symptoms of poverty, and of general misfortune and demoralization, whether of rich or poor. His conception of the Christian ministry was broad and thorough, and he wanted his cathedral to become the focus of the activities of all his ministers, clerical and lay, imparting the consecration of the altar to occupations that too often are scattered and unconscious of such consecration. He wanted the cathedral to be the "unifying centre" of all those activities of his people which are diocesan in their scope; and, so far as in him lay, he hoped to make it a symbol of that larger

Christian unity for which, to-day more than ever, the Christian denominations are praying and working. He wanted our Cathedral Chapter to foster the missionary spirit at home and abroad. Under the Bishop as the Chapter's head, he wanted us to be a college (in the original sense of the old Latin term) of learned, versatile, tactful, and sincere ministers of the faith of the Gospel, with diversities of gifts but the same Spirit; rightly dividing the word of truth; co-operating in good works; devoting our combined energies of study and reflection and prayer and ministration so as to put our Church and diocese in touch with the vast opportunities of this metropolis — with the wants alike of the toiling masses and of the learned and leisured few. He wanted our worship to be free for all and an education to all; uplifting; echoing and expressing day by day the appeal of Christ our Master: "Come unto Me, all ye that labor and are heavy laden, and I will give you rest. Take My yoke upon you, and learn of Me; for I am meek and lowly in heart: and ye shall find rest unto your souls. For My yoke is easy, and My burden is light."

All this our Bishop wanted of his Cathedral Chapter; and he wanted it, not as an artificial acquisition of his mind reflecting what others had desired and what he had elsewhere seen, but as the true expression of his own personality, the ideal which long experience had wrought in him as he grew in grace, and in the knowledge of our Lord and Saviour Jesus Christ.

Having felt hitherto the fascination of his presence, the impress of his mind in all these matters, we gather now to offer our grateful and respectful tribute to his distinguished memory; for God has called him to the larger life. Missing his familiar form, conscious of our loss, it is our duty and privilege to go forward in his spirit, and do our parts in the work which he laid upon us. That work shall be our constant reminder of him, until our day is done. And the harder we labor at our several tasks, the better shall we appreciate the scope and the devotion to duty of our great Bishop, who for twenty-five years bore on his shoulders a burden of responsibility and toil that would have overborne ten ordinary men. To the end he bore it well, and made no sign, until under the stress of it his physical strength suddenly gave way. To the very end his keen and hearty humor, his consideration for others, his cheeriness — he was the least worried person in his sickroom — his rare vitality, his broad interest in general affairs, and his indomitable patience prevailed.

To his wife and children we offer our respectful sympathy, praying that in God's good time, when the harvest is ready, we and they and he whom now we mourn may all be gathered into the heavenly garner. Grant him, O Lord, eternal rest, and may perpetual light shine on him.

THE REVEREND CANON LAURENCE HENRY SCHWAB

THE REVEREND CANON LAURENCE HENRY SCHWAB[1]

LAURENCE HENRY SCHWAB was born in New York in 1857, and was a son of Gustav Schwab and his wife Catherine Elizabeth von Post. He was graduated from Yale College in the class of 1878; and, after studying for Holy Orders at the Union Theological Seminary, New York, and at the Divinity School in Philadelphia, he was ordered deacon by Bishop Horatio Potter in 1881. He served as curate to the Rector of St. Michael's Church, New York, 1881-82. He was then ordered priest, and served at Grand Island, Nebraska, 1882-83; after which he was

---

[1] This minute was written at the request of the following Committee of the New York Clerical Club:
GEORGE WILLIAM DOUGLAS,
LORING W. BATTEN,
HENRY MOTTET.

associated with the Reverend Dr. William R. Huntington, as curate at All Saints' Church, Worcester, Massachusetts, 1883–84. Hence he passed successively to curacies in New York City at the Church of the Nativity, 1884–86, and at St. Mark's Chapel, 1886–88. In 1888 he became Rector of St. Mary's Church, Manhattanville; and, in 1899, of the Church of the Intercession, New York. Failing health compelled him to resign his rectorship in 1903; whereafter, for short periods, he took charge of churches at New Windsor, on the Hudson, and at Sharon, Connecticut. Meanwhile, on Bishop Henry C. Potter's nomination, he became a canon missioner at the Cathedral of St. John the Divine. He died on the Sunday after Ascension, May 28, 1911, leaving a widow and one son.

It is a short record, but full of significance to all who knew him. Both his first sermon and his last were delivered on Ascension Day; and in spite of constant physical weakness, his life was a continual ascension, mentally and spiritually, from strength to strength. This present account of him has specially to do with his association with this Club, which he valued greatly, and for which his fitness was recognized by us all. His utterances here, like his numerous articles in periodicals and newspapers, were characterized by scholarly tastes and intense mentality, which his modesty and fine reserve could not conceal. He was a born historian, and his mind was full of wide and just historical comparisons whereby his view of present concerns was illuminated, and any disposition to personal prejudice was sweetened and uplifted by a note of personal detachment. His piety was sincere and deep, for he was a man of prayer. These traits appeared in his sermons, which were more and more convincing, and more and more spiritual, as his brief life neared its earthly close. In familiar intercourse none could converse with him without being impressed by his rare integrity and truthfulness, by his exquisite purity, and by his affectionateness, wistful and gentle. Withal there was in his eye, and in his whole demeanor, a suggestion of the power of righteous wrath which the Psalmist includes in his portrait of the Good Man: "He doth abhor that which is evil" — the same trait which in the Apocalypse is attributed to the risen Jesus: "the wrath of the Lamb." Thus he seemed to have a better right than most of us to use, as he so constantly did, the language of St. Paul; for he was not afraid of all that is involved in the quest of righteousness and truth: he had counted the cost, and was ready for the sacrifice. To him the inner world was real, substantial; and Paul's zeal — the zeal of the climber from grace to grace — belonged to him by right of conquest.

He could not have been the minister of Christ to our time that he actually was — to, and in, our time — without experiencing religious difficulties on his own account. He knew and felt what Modernism means. Two years ago he volunteered to an intimate friend the information that at one time he had serious doubts as to one point of our Creed. He had troubles about prayer and God's answers to it. The Higher Criticism troubled him with fears that he might not be sure that he knew as much of the life and utterances of Jesus Christ as he had formerly believed that the New Testament declares. Nevertheless, he did not flinch; and to those who knew what went on in his soul, it was helpful to behold how he kept the faith. It was most appropriate that he had been commissioned by the family of Bishop Henry C. Potter to write his biography; for the Bishop admired and loved him, and he understood and loved the Bishop, and entered into the public spirit and the civic sense of that great citizen-churchman. But this task, like most of his other earthly tasks, Canon Schwab was compelled to leave unfinished — an uncompleted manuscript — to the great loss of our Church.

Perhaps the last touch of tragedy was given to his life by his inability to share our cathedral work just at the moment when the opportunities of it were enlarging for us all. That work appealed to the whole of him — to his historic information; to his instinct of social service; to his desire for a large Christian unity; to his sympathy with all sorts and conditions of men; to his yearning for great things for the spirit of man as the candle of the Lord; to his appreciation of worship in its noblest forms. But the joy and privilege of participating in our cathedral opportunities was, like so much else, withheld from him.

In conclusion, may we not lift the veil of privacy just far enough to say, as a simple sign of his natural affiliation with all things human, that he came to his death on this wise? The Friday after Ascension Day and his last sermon at the cathedral, he returned to Sharon, apparently in good health for him. As usual he had spent Sunday evening with his wife, each quietly reading. About nine o'clock he stepped out on the veranda of his cottage to breathe the fresh air and look at the stars, and to make sure that his pet dog was all right for the night. There, without warning, he was taken with a hemorrhage. His wife lifted him back into the room, but he soon lost consciousness, and in less than an hour he passed to his long home.

Shall we say that the struggle naught availed? He knew, and knows, better than that. To those whom he allowed to share his inner life he brought his own conviction home: that failure and falling short are no ground for despair: that, as Browning puts it, at last Paracelsus sees; since with God there is no waste. God gathers up the fragments, and the reapers are the angels.

NEWMAN ONCE MORE:
A STUDY

NEWMAN ONCE MORE:
A STUDY

I

Do you remember Schumann's bit of music which he entitled *Warum* — Why? — that elusive snatch of poignant, plaintive melody, which expresses a soul's surprise over the mysterious problem of its life? I can think of no better motto for Cardinal Newman's life, as it is portrayed in Wilfred Ward's recent volumes.[1]

This article is not intended as a critique of the latest biography of Newman, but rather as an expression of certain feelings and impressions with which I have laid the volumes down. As one thinks of that marvellous career as a whole, one wonders why Newman's unique personality was

---

[1] "The Life of John Henry, Cardinal Newman," by Wilfred Ward. 2 volumes. Longmans, 1912.

so winning yet so unhappy, so widely influential yet so abortive. From early youth to extreme old age this man of extraordinary vitality possessed, by common consent, the very genius of religion. "God was in all his thoughts." This personal recollection of God reinforced and fructified all his other powers, tinged his literary style, and was the secret of his influence. Others might *tell* us, but he made us *feel* that for each of us there is, in substance, but one life to live — the life with God. "As the eyes of a maiden unto the hand of her mistress, even so his eyes waited upon the Lord our God." From early youth, he writes, "I believed that the inward conversion of which I was conscious (and of which I am still more certain than that I have hands and feet) would last into the next life, and that I was elected to eternal glory. This belief helped in confirming me in my mistrust of the reality of material phenomena, and making me rest in the thought of two, and two only, absolute and luminously self-evident beings — myself and my Creator." [1] And far on toward middle age, in his "Grammar of Assent," he speaks of "the reality of conversion as cutting at the root of doubt, providing a chain between God and the soul that is with every link complete. I know I am right. How do you know it? I know that I know." [2] Furthermore, all his life long, under whatever circumstances, he was conscious that he had a mission in the world — "a great work to do in England." Why, then, was he so continuously unhappy, without and within? and why, from any standpoint of earthly results, did he so continuously fail? In spite of

---

[1] Vol. I., p. 30.   [2] "Grammar of Assent," p. 197.

his splendid popularity — of the multitudes who loved him, and were grateful to him, though they never even saw him — why, from first to last, did he arouse such antagonism? And why, at stage after stage, from his own point of view — from the standpoint of his intentions and overt aims — was his life, not only so sad, but so ineffectual? Why did he puzzle people in general? and why were most of his best friends always uneasy about him? For it would seem as if, of all his many friends, only three were never really uneasy about him, and always elicited his absolute confidence — gave him, in the human sense, entire satisfaction: Frederick Rogers and R. W. Church and Ambrose St. John — two of them Anglicans to the last; the third an Anglican who went over to the Church of Rome with Newman, and was with him in the Oratory. Of course, in the first place, it is a case of "The Hour and the Man." The Tractarian Movement, as a whole, shows that the Church of England was ready for Newman. The epoch found a voice in him — something which neither Keble nor Palmer nor Pusey could say, he had to say; and England wanted to have it said, even though Newman himself had hardly said it before he changed his mind and moved on further than England could follow.

But if we would understand and do justice to Newman as a personality, and if we would explain why his influence has been so helpful to ourselves, our analysis of his character and career must be deeper and more intimate. Our question therefore resolves itself into three, each of which is equally applicable throughout the two great divisions of his career, first in the Church of England, and afterwards in the Roman Catholic Church.

First, why was Newman's life not only so abortive of the results which he intended, but so out of harmony, at every stage, with his immediate surroundings?

Secondly, why did he so constantly puzzle his associates and arouse such personal antagonism, although he was so greatly admired?

Thirdly, why, nevertheless, was Newman's personal influence in his generation so pervasive and so powerful? and what was the real nature of his influence?

Someone has remarked of Hamlet that the reason why Shakespeare's play has held the stage is, that Hamlet is inscrutable. Newman is elusive, but he is not inscrutable, in the sense of Hamlet; and the more one ponders his life and writings, the more one seems to find a sufficient explanation of him.

Newman was perpetually out of agreement with his surroundings, whether Anglican or Roman Catholic, because he was by nature one of the most individual persons that ever lived. His aloofness was as instinctive as his insight was thorough. No matter whom he might be thrown with, he reacted. He could not but play a lone hand. He had it in him to be a leader of men, but at every crisis he sacrificed his leadership to his determination to stand alone. In all human movements party combinations are generally necessary in order to accomplish practical results; but Newman could not work with any party — could not "give to a party what was meant for mankind."

As Father Ryder puts it, "he had too keen a sense of individuality to enforce the necessary drill." What he wrote to Sister Maria Pia, in his sixty-ninth year, is an accurate description of his whole career:[1] "Like St. Gregory Nazianzen, I like going on my own way, and having my time my own. . . . Put me into official garb, and I am worth nothing; leave me to myself, and every now and then I shall do something. Dress me up, and you will soon have to make my shroud — leave me alone and I shall live my appointed time. Now do take this in, as a sensible nun." His own verse, "Thou couldst a people raise, but couldst not rule," was applicable to himself, he tells us.[2] His sympathies were of the strongest and sweetest, and his ability to understand and appreciate another's point of

---
[1] Vol. II., p. 281.   [2] Vol. II., p. 353.

view was extraordinarily keen; but his personal independence was indomitable. In this respect his own description of himself was accurate: "He rested in the thought of two, and two only, absolute and luminously self-evident beings — himself and his Creator." Hence his strong objection to those who, as he expressed it, "strove to narrow the terms of communion," [1] and unduly to curtail among Roman Catholics the liberty of thought which he believed to be the Catholic's birthright. He thought of every Christian as in the same direct relation with God as he himself was; and therefore his sense of shortcomings and imperfections which God permits within the Church no more impaired his conviction of the Church's divine mission, than his sense of the evil in the world diminished his certainty of

[1] Vol. I., p. 24.

God's providence. He was not intolerant of wide differences within the Christian pale. Within large limits he wanted to live and let live. In this regard his complaint, first against the Anglican Church authorities and afterwards against the Roman Catholic authorities, was the same: that they had no use for some of the best and most loyal children of the Church. What he said against the Church of England, in his sermon on "The Parting of Friends," was quite consistent with what he repeatedly said later against the Church of Rome. In his judgment neither the one nor the other encouraged free debate among loyal experts. "Truth is wrought out," he said, "by many minds working freely together."[1] "It is individuals, and not the Holy See, that have taken the initia-

---

[1] Vol. I., p. 23. Cp. II., p. 49.

tive and given the lead to the Catholic mind in theological inquiry."[1] For his own part, he believed that he was claiming for himself no other welcome than had been willingly accorded for centuries to freedom of debate in the mediæval schools as to the problems of their time; and it was because he nowhere obtained for himself such freedom — the freedom which he was eager to accord to his fellow-Churchmen — that, wherever he was, all his life long there was a note of discord. He must still go on wistfully seeking the home welcome which haply none of us shall completely find, till we arrive at "the Jerusalem above, which is free, the mother of us all." Whether, if he could have foreseen that he would be as lonely in the Roman Church as he was in the Anglican, he would ever have left the

[1] Vol. II., p. 39.

Anglican Church, is an unanswerable inquiry. Liddon and Pusey and Keble and R. W. Church conjectured that he would not; but no one can be sure. Probably it was a matter that would have been determined by his decision as to whether the sacrament of Holy Communion, as administered in the Church of England, did, or did not, assure to him the presence of Christ.[1] In John Inglesant, Mr. Shorthouse gives us an imaginary portrait of one who found the sacramental presence as truly in the English as in the Roman rite. Whether Newman could have been an Inglesant we shall never know. But it is impossible not to raise the question when, as late as 1868, we come across Canon Irvine's pathetic description of his unexpected meeting with Newman at Littlemore, as

---

[1] Cp. Vol. I., p. 577.

the aged priest was visiting unbeknown his old home:[1]

"I was passing by the church at Littlemore when I observed a man very poorly dressed leaning over the lych gate crying. He was to all appearances in great trouble. He was dressed in an old gray coat with the collar turned up and his hat pulled down over his face as if he wished to hide his features. As he turned toward me I thought it was a face I had seen before. The thought instantly flashed through my mind it was Dr. Newman. I had never seen him, but I remembered Mr. Crawley had got a photo of Dr. Newman. I went and told Mr. Crawley I thought Dr. Newman was in the village, but he said I must be mistaken, it could not be. I asked him to let me see the photo, which he did. I then told him I felt sure it was [he]. Mr. Crawley wished me to have another look at him. I went and met him in the churchyard. He was walking with Mr. St. John. I made bold to ask him if

[1] Vol. II., p. 206.

he was not an old friend of Mr. Crawley's, because if he was I felt sure Mr. Crawley would be very pleased to see him; as he was a great invalid and not able to get out himself, would he please to go and see Mr. Crawley? He instantly burst out crying and said, 'Oh no, oh no!' Mr. St. John begged him to go, but he said, 'I cannot.' Mr. St. John asked him then to send his name, but he said, 'Oh no!' At last Mr. St. John said, 'You may tell Mr. Crawley Dr. Newman is here.'"

With this clue — the indomitable individuality of the man — we can follow his course without confusion, and we can understand why three of his friends at least were never fundamentally perplexed about him. When he turns to Frederick Rogers, or to R. W. Church, or to Father St. John, he always finds that they have the same confidence as ever in his intellectual and moral sincerity, and "*cor ad cor loquitur.*" To the end they manifested to him the trust and forbearance and sympathetic comprehension which it had always been Newman's dream to find in his ecclesiastical superiors, but which, whether in the Anglican or in the Roman Church, he generally failed to obtain. For these three friends of his perceived that from crisis to crisis his course throughout was like a series of the subtlest chemical reactions, in which he was fundamentally consistent with himself. Newman was always Newman. Gladstone brought this out far on in Newman's career as a Roman Catholic, when, in their discussion about Vaticanism and the Pope's Infallibility, Gladstone pushed Newman to the wall and drew from him this confession: "If I am obliged to bring religion into after-dinner toasts (which indeed does not seem quite the thing), I shall drink, — to the Pope, if you please, — still to conscience first, and to the Pope afterwards." [1] Private judgment was still, as always, to Newman the most sacred function of the human soul — the ultimate court of appeal — "providing," as he said in the passage already quoted from his "Grammar of Assent," "a chain between God and the soul that is with every link complete. I know I am right. How do you know it? I know that I know." Nor did he have merely the courage to assert this to a Protestant: he advocated it also in controversy with Roman Catholics. Witness his article in the *Rambler*, "On Consulting the Faithful in Matters of Doctrine," to which, in a letter to Sir John Acton, June 20, 1860, he alludes thus: [2] "I wrote an Article on the right of the Laity to be consulted; and, as you

---

[1] Vol. II., p. 404.   [2] Vol. I., p. 636, cp. I., p. 502.

know, I thereby incurred a good deal of odium. It was this defence of the rights of the Laity which was the chief cause of the Bishop's dissatisfaction with me." Witness again, what he wrote in "The Grammar of Assent," in 1870, when he was sixty-nine years old:[1]

"Conscience . . . is always what the sense of the beautiful is in certain cases; it is always emotional. No wonder then that it always implies what that sense only sometimes implies; that it always involves the recognition of a living object, toward which it is directed. Inanimate things cannot stir our affections; these are correlative with persons. If, as is the case, we feel responsibility, are shamed, are frightened, at transgressing the voice of conscience, this implies that there is One to whom we are responsible, before whom we are ashamed, whose claims upon us we fear. If, on doing wrong, we feel the same tearful, broken-hearted sorrow

[1] Vol. II., p. 265.

which overwhelms us on hurting a mother; if, on doing right, we enjoy the same sunny serenity of mind, the same soothing, satisfactory delight which follows on our receiving praise from a father, we certainly have within us the image of some person, to whom our love and veneration look, in whose smile we find our happiness, for whom we yearn, toward whom we direct our pleadings, in whose anger we are troubled and waste away. These feelings in us are such as require for their exciting cause an intelligent being: 'The wicked flees, when no one pursueth'; then why does he flee? whence his terror? Who is it that he sees in solitude, in darkness, in the hidden chambers of his heart? If the cause of these emotions does not belong to this visible world, the Object to which his perception is directed must be Supernatural and Divine."

Yet Newman's disappointment at not finding anywhere at the hands of his fellow-men the reception that he wanted, was as naïve as that of a child. To the end of his career he was "a prisoner of hope," though his hopefulness lost its original buoyancy after the failure of his plans for a university in Ireland and for a Roman Catholic college at Oxford.

"I have generally got on well with juniors, but not with superiors," he writes concerning Manning.[1] "As to the Oxford scheme, it is still the blessed will of God to send me baulks. On the whole, I suppose, looking through my life as a course, He is using me, but really viewed in its separate parts it is but a life of failures."[2] "Well, facts alone will make them recognize the fact of what a laity must be in the nineteenth century if it is to cope with Protestantism."[3] "The Anglican Church has been a most useful breakwater against scepticism. . . . At present it upholds far more truth in England than any other form of religion would, and than the Roman Catholic Church could."[4]

---

[1] Vol. II., p. 87.
[2] Vol. II., p. 67.
[3] Vol. II., p. 69.
[4] Vol. I., p. 651.

"There has been a tradition among the Italians that the lay mind is barbaric — fierce and stupid — and is destined to be outwitted, and that fine craft is the true weapon of Churchmen. When I say the lay mind, I speak too narrowly — it is the Saxon, Teuton, Scandinavian, French mind."[1] "But the Latin race will not always have a monopoly of the magisterium of Catholicism."[2]

While he was an Anglican, Newman's instinctive disposition to react against his surroundings, whatever they might be, manifested itself first toward the Evangelicals; although to the end of his life some of their phrases and forms of thought were habitual with him. Next, while England was seething with the new thought of natural science, Newman was prompted to revive in Churchmen the standards and the spirit of the primitive Church. Hence he was a contributor to

---

[1] Vol. II., p. 141. [2] Vol. II., p. 555.

the Tracts for the Times, although in them he played a lone hand, as usual, and was a thorn in the side of Palmer, who originated the Tracts. Ere long it became evident that for Newman the primitive Church principles, as he understood them, were insufficient; and, by way of farther reaction, he must superimpose on them some mediæval habits of mind; by which combination of primitive with mediæval ratiocination, he tried to find the Via Media which seemed to him to be the intention of the Church of England at the Reformation. But in this neither Conservatives nor Liberals could run far with him; and so the first act of his life's drama was concluded — a drama, but not a tragedy, when we consider, on the one hand, the wonderful revival of personal religion, and of attachment to the Church of England, to which Newman's genius for piety had contributed; and, on the other hand, the exquisite beauty of character and humility of spirit which Newman's painful conflict had developed in himself. For, in spite of some superficial appearances to the contrary, he had become humble. In him we find a man who, though egotistical, could be humble because he was unselfish. He had the charity which seeketh not her own. In his verses from Italy, "Lead, kindly Light," written just before the Tractarian Movement had begun, as Newman looked backward over his early years he confessed, "Pride ruled my will"; but by the time when he delivered his sermon on "The Parting of Friends," he had grown to be truly humble. He went on exercising his private judgment with the same integrity; but he had counted the cost, and he did so ever afterward as a bravely humble man.

"With me it is a very small thing that I should be judged of you, or of man's judgment: yea, I judge not mine own self. He that judgeth me is the Lord."

Thus the key to his perpetual hopefulness, on the one hand, and to his perpetual discouragement and distress, on the other hand, is his indomitable individuality, exercised throughout his long life in the sphere of pure religion. I have always detected a resemblance in Newman to Ralph Waldo Emerson. Early in the Tractarian days, John Anthony Froude compared Newman to Julius Cæsar:[1]

"He was above middle height, slight and spare. His head was large, his face remarkably like that of Julius Cæsar. The forehead, the shape of the ears and nose were almost the same. The lines of the mouth

---

[1] "Newman's Biography," Vol. I., p. 61.

were very peculiar, and I should say exactly the same. I have often thought of the resemblance, and believed that it extended to the temperament. In both there was an original force of character which refused to be moulded by circumstances, which was to make its own way, and become a power in the world; a clearness of intellectual perception, a disdain for conventionalities, a temper imperious and wilful, but along with it a most attaching gentleness, sweetness, singleness of heart and purpose. Both were formed by nature to command others, both had the faculty of attracting to themselves the passionate devotion of their friends and followers. It has been said that men of letters are either much less or much greater than their writings. . . . A man of genius, on the other hand, is a spring in which there is always more behind than flows from it. . . . This was eminently true of Newman. Greatly as his poetry had struck me, he was himself all that the poetry was, and something far beyond. I had then never seen so impressive a person. . . . Nothing was too large for him, nothing too trivial, if it threw light upon the central question, what man really was, and what was his destiny."

In other words, transport Julius Cæsar into the England of the nineteenth century; make him utterly unworldly — caring for nothing but the fortunes of the human soul: devoted to God and the duties of the soul with passionate intensity — and you have Newman whether in the Church of England or in the Church of Rome. He is an instance of profound and pure spiritual passion, as pure as possible for man. He thought himself impartial, but no human being can be quite impartial and also profoundly impassioned — only the Perfect Man, the God-Man on the Cross, has displayed to mankind the combination of perfect impartiality to the truth, with perfect passion for the truth. Yet there must be passion in every genuine intellectual leader of men.

In this respect Newman reminds us of Count Paul von Hoensbroech's account of himself in the Introduction to his thrilling narrative, "Fourteen Years a Jesuit," where he says:[1]

"But though my judgment is impartial, its expression will not be dispassionate, for passion only dims our vision and weakens our judgment when it takes possession of us before the object has been grasped by our vision and understanding. When we have recognized and understood, then we may call in its aid. Indeed, it would be well if conviction were more frequently upheld with passion. There would be less uncertainty, weakness, and insincerity in the world. Many a good book would not have missed its effect had it been written with more of passion. How indeed would it be possible to write dispassionately about that which has stirred our souls to their depths?"

---

[1] Vol. I., p. xiv. Introduction. "Fourteen Years a Jesuit," by Count Paul von Hoensbroech, translated by Alice Zimmern. Cassell & Co., New York, 1911.

II

Not long after Newman had gone over to Rome, Charles Kingsley — bluff John Bull personified — accused him, in substance, of duplicity and jesuitry. By his inquiry, "What then does Dr. Newman mean?" Kingsley signified that Newman was not frank: that he always had something at the back of his head which he did not tell. But in the judgment of English people generally Newman's "Apologia" disposed of this charge entirely. Newman's reply to Kingsley was certainly an exhibition of his incomparable intellectual dexterity; but it showed him to be what R. W. Church and Rogers and St. John always believed him to be — quite sincere and outspoken — a transparent character. He always meant what he said; and usually his rare gift of expression and illustration enabled him to say what he meant. Now and then indeed, like all persons who write rapidly, his language was obscure; and like all who are very shy, he sometimes trusted too much that his correspondent would read between the lines. His letter to Bishop Ullathorne [1] about coming to Rome for the Cardinal's hat was of this kind. But in general the trouble was that, intellectually, he was not only subtle and keenly sensitive to his immediate environment, but he was always on the move, — backwards or forwards according to the occasion. Even his sermons were occasional, and he was a prolific letter-writer. It is said that great judges avoid writing many letters lest their casual opinions should conflict with their formal decisions. But Newman, even in his books, was occa-

[1] Vol. II., p. 439.

sional. From moment to moment he expressed his mind, but he continually changed his mind, or passed to another point of view; and at every move he abounded in striking arguments for his new position. Hereby he bewildered slow-moving minds; and to Kingsley he appeared to be — not like a bird moving rapidly in the sunshine — but a chameleon, standing still and changing his color in order to elude the observer. Kingsley did not recognize that whether Newman's statements were objectively true or not, they were subjectively true: that he was not concealing, but uttering his mind.

Perhaps, paradoxical as it may appear, the best proof of Newman's absolute truthfulness was an incidental one: his unwillingness to proselytize. For this the Romanists never forgave him. Just at first it looked as if he might do what had been expected of him. Yielding to the natural desire to keep with him some of his dearest friends, he did try to induce Henry Wilberforce and a few others to join him at once in the Church of Rome.[1] But he soon resumed his instinctive aloofness. Thus as early as 1850 he writes to Mr. Capes:

"As far as the *people* are concerned our line is not to attack the Church of England, which is a low game." [2]

Again in 1860 he writes to Canon Estcourt:

"I should have the greatest repugnance to introducing controversy into those quiet circles and sober schools of thought which are the strength of the Church of England. It is another thing altogether to introduce controversy to individual minds which are already unsettled, or have a drawing toward Catholicism. Altogether another thing in a

---

[1] Vol. I., pp. 133–134; 618.   [2] Vol. I., p. 261.

place like Birmingham, where nearly everyone is a nothingarian, or an infidel, a sceptic, or an inquirer. Here Catholic efforts are not only good in themselves, and do good, but cannot possibly do any even incidental harm — here whatever is done is so much gain. In Oxford you would unsettle many, and gain a few, if you did your most." [1]

In 1864 he writes to R. W. Church:

"I can truly say, and never will conceal, that I have no wish at all to do anything against the Establishment while it is a body preaching dogmatic truth, as I think it does at present." [2]

But the very trait which attested his fastidious sincerity, and his respect for the mind of others, led the Romanists to distrust him for not being really one of themselves. They had hailed his arrival in their midst, because they expected him to be the first-born of many brethren.

---

[1] Vol. II., pp. 57, 58.   [2] Vol. II., p. 24.

If he believed in Romanism why did he not bestir himself, and wield his magic wand, and throw his subtle net, until all the good Anglicans had been drawn after him to Rome? When Romanists found that Newman would on no account play this rôle, they entertained almost the same distrust of him that Kingsley had; so that at the very time when the Anglicans were coming to trust Newman, though he had gone from them, the Romanists lost confidence in him, although he had come to them. They could not perceive that he was as genuine and naïve as ever, and that he had come to Rome for his own reasons, not for theirs: that, as he wrote to Canon Estcourt, "Catholics did not make us Catholics; Oxford made us Catholics."[1] The fact was that he had come to Rome as an idealist, not as a realist — as a Pla-

---
[1] Vol. II., p. 57; cp. Vol. II., pp. 110–127.

tonist, not as an Aristotelian; and his conviction was that Rome was not yet ready for most Anglicans, any more than most Anglicans were ready for Rome. As he had formerly believed that "there was a great work for him to do in England," so now he believed there was a great work for him to do in Rome. Newman was still Newman, reacting against his environment as of old. He was now bent on reforming the Roman communion, just as sincerely as formerly he had been bent on reforming the Anglican communion. Yet can we altogether wonder that Monsignor Talbot was amazed when, in reply to the invitation which, with the Pope's backing, he sent to Newman, to come from England and preach to Protestant visitors in Talbot's church in Rome, the following tart reply was received:

"The Oratory, Birmingham, July 25, 1864.

"Dear Monsignore Talbot, — I have received your letter, inviting me to preach next Lent in your church at Rome to 'an audience of Protestants more educated than could ever be the case in England.'

"However, Birmingham people have souls; and I have neither taste nor talent for the sort of work which you cut out for me. And I beg to decline your offer.

I am, yours truly,
JOHN H. NEWMAN."[1]

So Newman failed in Rome as he had failed in England, and for a similar cause. The Romanists did not relish his attitude, and they were suspicious of his arguments, like the Trojans with the Greeks. Even when he offered them new arms against the heretics — arms which he himself often wielded effectively — they doubted whereunto this would grow. Newman desired to convert men by the instrument of thought,[2] whereas the Ultramontanes preferred to influence them by other instruments than thought. So,

---

[1] Vol. II., p. 539.   [2] Vol. I., p. 122.

though at first they approved his project of making a new translation of the Scriptures (with Newman's scholarship and rare gift of style and sense of rhythm, how interesting such a translation might have been!), they soon discouraged it, and it came to nothing. As the wretched years went by, time and again the support which had been promised him from headquarters silently slipped away. Each enterprise in which he had thought that he saw God's hand guiding him, and on which he had set his heart, came to naught; and now and then his grief finds some such bitter record as this:

"People do not know me — and sometimes they half pass me by. It has been the portion of saints, even; and well may be my portion. He who gives gifts is the best judge how to use His own. He has the sole right to do as He will, and He knows what He is doing. Yet sometimes it is marvellous to me how my life is going, and I have never been brought out prominently — and now I am likely less than ever — for there seems something of an iron form here, tho' I may be wrong; but I mean people are at no trouble to deepen their views. It is natural."[1] "I am treated as some wild, incomprehensible beast, a spectacle for Dr. Wiseman to exhibit to strangers, as himself being the hunter who captured it."[2] "They put me on the shelf, but they can't prevent me from peeping out from it."[3]

Again in his diary:

"'Not understood' — this is the point. I have seen great wants which had to be supplied among Catholics — especially as regards education — and of course those who labored under those wants did not know their state, — and did not see or understand the want of all — or what was the supply of the want — and felt no thankfulness at all, and no consideration towards a person who was doing something toward the supply; but

---

[1] Vol. I., p. 173. [2] Vol. I., p. 569. [3] Vol. I., p. 573.

rather thought him restless or crotchety, or in some way or other what he should not be. This made me think of turning more to God, if it has not actually turned me. It has made me feel that in the Blessed Sacrament is my great consolation, and that, while I have Him Who lives in the Church, the separate members of the Church, my superiors, though they may claim my obedience, have no claim on my admiration, and offer nothing for my inward trust. I have expressed this feeling, or, rather, implied it, in one of my Dublin sermons, preached in 1856. So far well — or not ill — but it so happens that, contemporaneously with this neglect on the part of those for whom I labored, there has been a drawing toward me on the part of Protestants. Those very books and labors of mine which Catholics do not understand, Protestants did. Moreover, by a coincidence, things I had written years ago, as a Protestant, and the worth or force of which were not understood by Protestants then, are bearing fruit among Protestants now. . . . And accordingly I have been attracted by that sympathy to desire more of that sympathy, feeling lonely and fretting under, not so much the coldness toward me (though that in part) as the ignorance, narrowness of mind, and self-conceit of those whose faith and virtue and goodness, nevertheless, I at the same time recognized. And thus I certainly am under the temptation of looking out for, if not courting, Protestant praise." [1]

How truly he had described himself when he wrote to Mr. Hutton [2] that nothing could be said about him, in praise or blame, which did not "tear off his morbidly sensitive skin"; for he had the artistic temperament. Toward the close of his life he spoke of Tertullian as one of his two favorites — as the theological genius — among the early Fathers of the Church; adding, says Father Ryder, "with tears in his voice, if not in his eyes, how frequently the initial sin of heresy

---
[1] Vol. I., pp. 577, 578. [2] Vol. I., p. 20.

was impatience."[1] Was this a hit at himself? If it was, then Newman was now saying to himself what Keble had long before said for him:

"Why should we faint, or fear to live alone,
  Since all alone, so Heaven has willed, we die,
Nor even the tenderest heart, and next our own
  Knows half the reasons why we smile and sigh?"[2]

Meanwhile he clung to life to the end. Father Neville writes:[3]

"He knew how he would be missed by some, and he felt for them; and there were objects and interests which he held very tenderly in mind with this thought of them — what would happen in the struggle which in his forecast of the future seemed likely to come? God's cause was ever in his mind. And as long as he could in any way serve it he desired to stay."

---

[1] Vol. II., p. 354.
[2] "The Christian Year," Twenty-fourth Sunday after Trinity.
[3] Vol. II., p. 536.

The fact was that to the great majority of Roman Catholics he was not merely uncongenial — that to their excessive dogmatism his tendency to minimize was irksome, and to their imperialism he seemed too democratic — besides this, many Anglicans and very many Roman Catholics considered that he was substantially a sceptic. Dr. Fairbairn expresses this estimate: "He has a deep distrust of the intellect; he dares not trust his own, for he does not know where it might lead him, and he will not trust any other man's. 'The Grammar of Assent' is pervaded by the intensest philosophical scepticism."[1] Such critics fail, I think, to see the difference between scepticism and the ability to enter into the mind of the sceptic — to imagine him as a concrete reality, an actual human being. New-

---
[1] Vol. II., p. 505.

man himself, as we have already noticed, had indeed declared that up to the time of his conversion, as he was going up to Oxford in 1817, he was conscious of a strong intellectual tendency to scepticism,[1] and he thanked God that He shielded him morally from what intellectually might easily have come on him; — which is equivalent to saying that in early years his philosophical position was in this respect like Kant's. But whether the Kantian position can be properly termed sceptical, or not, at any rate from the time of his conversion Newman was in this respect a changed man: he was not essentially a sceptic; for he held that God was the starting-point and stay of all his thinking, and he loved God with his mind.[2] Nor was he sceptical about the Church;

---

[1] Vol. I., p. 31.
[2] Vol. I., p. 30; cp. Vol. II., p. 265.

he believed in the Church's divinity. But he was keenly alive to the human element in the Church, and frightened his friends by the intellectual vividness and the moral earnestness with which he apprehended this human element. In this regard his intellectual and moral perceptions were as keen as was the fastidiousness of his palate. (In his Oriel days this abstemious man had been selected to taste the wines for the college cellar.) He was aware of the physical and psychological and subconscious forces that are at work in the human mind. He knew that the best of logic is ineffective when the intellectual instrument of the indivisible man is out of working order. Around God as the central Object, his active mind was always on the move; but, according to his own attestation near the end of his life, from the moment of his conversion he never once had been sceptical about God's reality, nor about his own absolute relation to God, as of person to Person. Surely Newman, rather than any other man, is the proper judge as to whether this is the true account of himself. "For a man's mind is sometime wont to tell him more than seven watchmen, that sit above in a high tower."[1] Newman's sensitive, elastic, nimble mind moved too fast and too far for others to keep up with him: his utterances, while not indicative of scepticism on his part, did doubtless appear sceptical to others; for if others had said what he said, they would have been sceptics; but Newman's own faith was firm. He loved God with all his mind and heart and soul and strength. He was conscious of shortcomings and infirmities, and did

---

[1] Ecclus. xxxvii. 14.

not try to hide them; but we must accept his own account of himself on the score of scepticism. The bottom quality of Newman's thought, and therefore of his style (for in his case the style is the man), was that in theology he would not abandon the scientific method upon an ethical impulse. He wanted, like Wordsworth's cloud, to "move altogether if he moved at all." Even in his abstract thinking he insisted upon holding on to both the scientific and the ethical impulse; so that he appeared sceptical to those who sacrificed the scientific to the ethical. He dreaded the ecclesiastical narrowness that will not face the facts of science and of modern civilization. "There is," he wrote to Sir Frederick Rogers, "in particular quarters a narrowness which is not of God."[1] Newman's point of view was, first,

---
[1] Vol. I., p. 439.

that cold reason is by no means always on the side of science, any more than mysticism is always absent from scientific thinking; and secondly, that some of the primary perceptions and movements of the intellect are quite as authoritative acts as are some of our ethical decisions. Here was the point of Newman's conversion in his seventeenth year; and his whole subsequent course and influence depended on it. Newman was determined to pursue a rational method in pursuit of religious ideals. In his theology, faith was not a renunciation of reason: authority and inquiry were reconcilable; whereas, to many, faith and reason are not reconcilable: *credo quia impossible;* and to such persons Newman appeared to be a sceptic. But to his own Master he standeth or falleth; and we, his fellows on the transcendental way, must, in this respect, take him at his word.

An excellent illustration of Newman's method is furnished by his determination to minimize the Pope's Infallibility; and strangely enough this is the one instance in his whole career where he succeeded in his immediate object of endeavor; and the Cardinal's hat was his reward for this, since Leo XIII., unlike his successor, the present Pope, sympathized with Newman's attitude as a minimizer. To begin with, Newman did not want the dogma of Infallibility to be promulgated by a Council. He wanted to let well alone. He would allow to the Pope Infallibility as an abstraction; which would be about equivalent to saying that while the Pope's private judgment was doubtless better than his own, he wished the Pope to be enough of a gentleman to keep his private judgment pretty much to himself. If, in deference to the desires of other Roman Catholics, Newman were called to go further than this, and to admit the Pope's Infallibility as an abstract proposition generally binding on the faithful, in that case Newman, and every other intelligent Roman Catholic, must be allowed to interpret and apply the proposition after his own fashion; and if there must be a conciliar proclamation of the proposition, Newman was bound to be allowed to apply to it a minimizing interpretation and to get general acceptance for his minimizing. In practical application it was to be explained away. In this endeavor Newman was, for the time being, successful. Manning and Ward were against him, and, in this case, Manning for the nonce joined hands with the Jesuits. Thus Newman was in England confronted with what he called, "an insolent and aggressive faction."[1] Furthermore, the Roman Catholic schools of Belgium, Holland, France, and Italy, under the direction of the religious orders, — true Ultramontanes almost all of them — were against Newman. Nevertheless, he won out. Canon Scott Holland, in *The Commonwealth*, has thus described the situation:[2]

"And there is the Holy Father himself, most lovable of men, but absolutely ignorant what the problem is which his own infallibility is required to solve; utterly ignorant of all the intellectual anxieties which are sweeping over the minds of the laity as Newman knows them; utterly unaware that there are such anxieties; utterly out of touch with the very situation which cries aloud for his infallible authority to act. He smiles and

---

[1] Vol. II., p. 289.
[2] *The Commonwealth* for March, 1912, pp. 82-83.

jokes his way along, and carries the Council with him to declare his infallibility, by sheer delight in his good-humored puns. And yet you love him all the time, and are amused to find that in the end he has passed the definition of his own infallibility in the contrary sense to the one which he himself intended. For certainly it has come out that the infallibility proclaimed is to be understood, not in the sense of the party who carried it, but in the sense of those minimizers whom they decried; so that instead of Mr. W. G. Ward's vision of a Papal Bull arriving every morning for your breakfast with *The Times* and toast, there has not been really one single infallible utterance in the forty years that have followed the proclamation."

Thus Newman and Lord Acton and Dupanloup and Montalembert and Lacordaire, and the Liberal Catholics generally, prevailed at last over Manning and Ward and Louis Veuillot and the Ultramontanes, to whose confusion Newman was presented with the hat of a Cardinal, by way of stopping people from saying that "the Pope snubbed him."[1]

But in all this Newman was Newman still, reacting as before against his surroundings and insisting on exercising his own indomitable individuality. In the old Tractarian days Newman had complained that the Bishops of the Church of England in matters of Christian dogma uttered no certain sound: now he complained that the universal Bishop of Christendom was too certain in his utterances. In his Roman Catholic surroundings Newman wanted greater freedom of utterance and interpretation for himself; and for the moment his efforts as a minimizer were crowned with Pope Leo's approval. But it was only for a little while. How

---
[1] Vol. II., p. 445.

completely Newman failed in persuading the Roman Catholic communion to stand for what he stood for, is sufficiently disclosed by Pope Pius X.'s Encyclical of Feb. 11, 1906, where these words occur: "As for the multitude, their only duty is to let themselves be led, and to follow their Shepherd as a docile herd."

III

It has often been remarked that after he joined the Roman Catholic Church, Newman passed, intellectually, under an eclipse. This is hardly exact, for his "Difficulties of Anglicans," "Apologia," and "Grammar of Assent" are as brilliant, and in some respects as valuable, as any of his productions; his "Dream of Gerontius" is a poem of fine imagination and great spiritual power; and his "Essay on the Development of Christian Doctrine" was epoch-making, if only because it was the precursor of Modernism, and profoundly influenced such men as Loisy and Father Tyrrell. But, with these exceptions, there does seem to be a steady decline in the quality of his productions, and the sermons published in his Roman Catholic days do not, for the most part, hold their own in comparison with the "Parochial" and the "University" sermons of his Anglican ministry. Perhaps one reason for this decline was the fact that this period of his life was shrouded in despondency. His portraits at this time are likenesses of a very unhappy man, and he had too much of the sensitive, artistic temperament to do justice to his natural talents under such conditions.

Meanwhile he presents to us an aspect which is perhaps more difficult to understand and analyze than any other of his many sides. Who that has appreciated the transparency of Newman's soul and the force of his intellect can follow with aught else than astonishment, during his later Roman Catholic period, his attitude in worship? We see him now passing into the Roman Catholic atmosphere of devotion, and here, as always, he is peculiar to himself. But what an extraordinary combination of elements and of points of view does he now present to us! The very sincerity of the man, and his rare ability to express the workings of his soul, render him more than ever elusive. Yet if we examine ourselves before we examine him, we shall recognize that even here we can and must go with him a certain distance: that at least there is a certain parallelism between what we find him doing and what we do in worship. For, though we Protestants are prone to forget it, there is, and always has been, and always must be, a measure of accommodation in the worship of all mankind. Before we charge Newman with being either intellectually, or else morally, impossible and inconsistent — before we assert that in his words and acts of devotion he is untrue to his own professed intellectual tenets, and to the moods of his abstract argumentation, — we Protestants must first consider carefully our own attitude and expressions when we pass from religious ratiocination to worship, whether public or private. Is there not accommodation in the worship of the most determined and self-repressed of Protestants? Is it not true of all men's words and acts of devotion that "these things are an allegory," "figures of the true"? "that now we see as in a mirror, darkly"? Both in Roman Catholic and in Protestant worship men have to accommodate themselves, first, to the forms and symbols and expressions of the past: we enter into the worship of our forefathers. Furthermore, from youth to age our worship is a continuous process of accommodation of our former selves to our present selves: the meaning to us of our forms of Divine Service varies with our years, and with our experience of God and of human life: each mature individual has to adapt himself, as he now is, to himself as he has been: he puts a new significance into the old acts and words; and even in full maturity he still, like his children who worship at his side, is dealing with symbols of the true, lifting up his heart unto the Lord. Again, we must accommodate ourselves to our neighbors: educated and uneducated, prince and pauper, in common worship must sing the same hymns, say the same prayers, perform the same acts. In this matter of comprehensive flexibility some good Protestants feel hardly less keenly than Newman the chilly rigidity of parts of the English Prayer Book — the remoteness of some of our Prayer Book services from the masses of the people. It is by no means impossible for us to understand Newman in his preference for the warmth and promiscuousness of the service of a great Roman Catholic cathedral. When he first left the Church of England he thus described to Henry Wilberforce his impression of the worship in St. Peter's, Rome: [1]

"I doubt if you will understand me, but a Catholic cathedral is a sort of world, everyone going about his own business, but that business a religious one; groups of worshippers, and solitary ones — kneeling, stand-

---

[1] Vol. I., pp. 140-141.

ing — some at shrines, some at altars — hearing Mass and communicating, currents of worshippers intercepting and passing by each other — altar after altar lit up for worship, like stars in the firmament — or the bell giving notice of what is going on in parts you do not see, and all the while the canons in the choir going through matins and lauds, and at the end of it the incense rolling up from the high altar, and all this in one of the most wonderful buildings in the world and every day — lastly, all of this without any show or effort — but what everyone is used to — everyone at his own work, and leaving everyone else to his.... It is always a refreshment to the mind, and elevates it, to enter a church such as St. Fidelis. It has such a sweet, smiling, open countenance — and the altar is so gracious and winning, standing out for all to see, and to approach. The tall polished marble columns, the marble rails, the marble floor, the bright pictures, all speak the same language. And a light dome crowns the whole. Perhaps I do but follow the way of elderly persons, who have seen enough that is sad [in] life to be able to dispense with officious, intentional sadness — and as the young prefer autumn and the old spring, the young tragedy and the old comedy, so in the ceremonial of religion, younger men have my leave to prefer Gothic, if they will but tolerate me in my weakness, which requires the Italian. It is so soothing and pleasant, after the hot streets, to go into these delicate yet rich interiors, which are like the bowers of paradise or an angel's chamber. We found the same in a different way in Paris. It was oppressively hot, and we wandered through the narrow streets in the evening, seeking out the Jesuits' house. When we found it, the Superior was out, and we were ushered in, as into a drawing-room, into so green and beautiful a garden, with refreshing trees on the lawn, and quiet figures stealing along the walks saying their office. We entered a trellised walk of vines and seated ourselves on a stone bench which lay on the ground."

Undoubtedly in Protestant congregations there are proportionately a larger number of educated people than in most Roman Catholic congregations; and the average Teutonic and Anglo-Saxon mind uses religious symbols more sparingly and with a greater faculty of abstraction than, for example, the average Italian; undoubtedly, furthermore, the habit of the more intellectual Italians to worship constantly with persons less educated and more childish than themselves induces even the more intellectual to consent to forms of worship which they themselves have intellectually outgrown, until finally their minds do not, as otherwise they might, rebel against such forms. A similar result may be seen among Protestants who worship in company with their children, in contrast to Protestants who do not even try to adjust themselves to their children in mind and soul. But a candid Protestant must admit that, however simple and undemonstrative his forms of public worship may be, if they are to appeal to and include the people generally, they must be characterized by comprehensive flexibility and a generous use of symbols, and of objects to assist devotion and guide the eye and fire the imagination, — in short, to exercise not merely the mind but the body also, and to relieve the soul. At bottom we are touching here the whole subject of idolatry; and any Protestant who has travelled in the Orient, or conversed with missionaries, or even visited social settlements in our own city slums, sooner or later comes to the conclusion that he must revise his definition of the term idolatry. Nay, before we have done with this deep, difficult question, many of us will be asking ourselves whether there are not many idols in Protestant homes, and in

Protestant minds that never bow down in prayer to wood or stone. Certainly Bacon decided that there are. On the other hand, one of our ablest American professors, who has made a study of childhood, declares his conviction that many savages, both children and adults, are not really as idolatrous as we are prone to suppose. In other words, education and the habit of dealing with intellectual theories and spiritual abstractions do not necessarily remove from even the most enlightened of us the temptation to worship false gods; and it was not for naught that an Old Testament prophet warned his people against "setting up idols in their heart." Especially in these days, when the widespread desire for Christian Unity is drawing the various denominations of Christians nearer to each other in faith and worship, must not the absolute necessity of revising our notions as to what will be required of us in this matter of accommodation in worship, be more than ever in our minds?

Recognizing, therefore, the complexity of this whole subject, when treated squarely and thoroughly, we shall be slow to accuse Newman of insincerity when he worships as ordinary Roman Catholics do, and even when he exercises his amazing ability to argue in their defence. Yet, no matter what parallelism there be between what Newman did and what we all do — mentally and spiritually, no less than by bodily signs and acts — in worship, nevertheless we cannot deny that before long Newman becomes to us "a lost leader." There are obscure and subconscious psychological processes through which Newman passes that we do not partake of; and his intellect, formerly so clear, is overcast with superstition. Nor can we fail to notice that even now, in the midst of his recently adopted Roman Catholic environment, Newman is still Newman — still going his own way, still reacting and asserting his individuality. On the one hand, he insists on exercising his Anglo-Saxon temperament — the habits of non-Latin mentality. Alluding to Faber and Ward and other recent and rabid converts to Rome, he writes:[1] "They are in no sense spokesmen for English Catholics, and they must not stand in the place of those who have a real title to such an office." When Dr. Pusey in his Eirenicon quoted from Roman Catholic manuals many extreme expressions of devotion to the Blessed Virgin Mary and the Saints, Newman replied:

---
[1] Vol. II., p. 104.

"Sentiments such as these I freely surrender to your animadversion; I never knew of them till I read your book, nor, as I think, do the vast majority of English Catholics know them. They seem to me like a bad dream."[1] "I prefer English habits of belief and devotion to foreign, for the same causes, and by the same right, which justifies foreigners in preferring their own."[2] "In England Catholics pray *before* images, not *to* them. I wonder whether as many as a dozen pray *to* them, but *they* will be the best Catholics, not ordinary ones. The truth is, that sort of affectionate fervor which leads one to confuse an object with its representation is skin-deep in the South and argues nothing for a worshipper's faith, hope, and charity, whereas in a Northern race, like ours, with whom ardent devotional feeling is not common, it may be the mark of great spirituality. As to the nature of the feeling itself, and its absolute incongruity with any intellectual intention of addressing the image as an image, I think it is not difficult for any one with

---

[1] Vol. II., p. 106.   [2] Vol. II., p. 110.

an ordinary human heart to understand it. Do we not love the picture which we may have of friends departed? Will not a husband wear in his bosom and kiss the miniature of his wife? Cannot you fancy a man addressing himself to it, as if it were the reality? Think of Cowper's lines on his Mother's picture. 'Those lips are thine,' he says, 'thy own sweet smile I see' — and then 'Fancy shall steep me in Elysian reverie, a momentary dream *that thou art She.*' And then he goes on to the picture, 'My Mother,' etc."[1]

On the other hand, how can a man like Newman, who still retains so much of the Anglo-Saxon mentality, and who was once indeed a Protestant — how can he — though he has become a Romanist and embraced Mariolatry and the worship of saints — how can he possibly be jocose about it, and, even when he is at his prayers to saints, indulge in persiflage? If we know ourselves at all,

[1] Vol. I., p 652.

in case we ever broke into such expressions as the following, it would mean that our prayers to saints were not real prayers. But Newman is so individual, and temperamentally so sincere, that he is, towards his patron saint, very much as we, in our years of discretion, are towards our earthly parents, whom we still respect and lean on, but at the same time criticise and now and then find fault with. In so great and wise and saintly a man as François de Sales there was a little of this, even in his attitude toward our Heavenly Father; for did he not, in all seriousness, write to one of his penitents, "If God tires you, tell Him that He tires you"? But toward the Virgin Mary and St. Philip, his patron saint, Newman goes much farther than that.

He writes to Sister Imelda:[1]

---

[1] Vol. I., pp. 288-289.

"I smiled at the cleverness with which you are attempting to get up a miraculous Image in England. Now as to your proposal, I have this difficulty, that it is taxing our Blessed Lady unfairly — not her power, but her willingness. . . . Now what right have I, for the sake of my private ends, to put your Image on trial? It has done everything for you, — because you have asked what you ought to ask. Now you wish me to ask a *very hard* thing, and that (in a way) *selfishly*, and you make me say to our Lady, 'Do it under pain of your Image losing its repute.' . . . It is just possible, and rather more than possible, that it is His blessed will that I should suffer — and though I don't think so quite so much as I did, yet somehow at first sight I do not like to be *unkind*, if I may use such a word, to your Image. . . . I will not get you into any more scrapes with Reverend Mother. I gladly avail myself of her offer — and promise that if her Madonna gains my acquittal I will gladly come to Clifton, preach a sermon in her honor, and, if it is consistent with your rules, carry her in procession. . . . Thank you with all my heart for what you are so kindly intending to gain for me. Thank you also for the reproof you have administered to me. I know well I am an unbelieving old beast; and so perhaps in this instance. Recollect, however, dear Reverend Mother, that our House in Birmingham is erected under the Invocation of the Immaculate Mother of God, as beseems an Oratory of St. Philip — and is dedicated to her forever, and that you will not please *her* by abusing *him*."

As to St. Philip Neri, and his shortcomings as a patron saint, this is how Newman expresses himself, not in a letter — as above about the Virgin Mary — but in a prayer to God Himself:[1]

"O my God, in Thy sight, I confess and bewail my extreme weakness in distrusting, if not Thee, at least Thy own servants and representatives, when things do not turn out as I would have them, or expected! Thou hast given me St. Philip, that great creation of Thy grace, for my master and patron —

[2] Vol. II., p. 365.

and I have committed myself to him — and he has done very great things for me, and has in many ways fulfilled toward me all that I can fairly reckon he had promised. But, because in some things he has disappointed me, and delayed, I have got impatient; and have served him, though without conscious disloyalty, yet with peevishness and coldness. O my dear Lord, give me a generous faith in Thee and in Thy servants!"

That is how he expressed himself in actual prayer to God concerning St. Philip; and in another place we have in one of Newman's letters to Father St. John, an instance of how Newman would remonstrate with St. Philip himself:[1]

"The case is different when I think of St. Philip; then I argue thus: There is just one virtue which he asks for, detachment, which at the same time he prevents me having. There is just one thing which hinders me being detached, and that is, that I have made

---
[1] Vol. II., pp. 345-346.

myself his servant. What wish have I for life, or for success of any kind, except so far as and because I have this his congregation on my hands? He it is who has implicated me in the world, in a way in which I never was before, or at least never since my mother died and my sisters married. For St. Philip's sake I have given up my liberty, and have, as far as the temptation and trial of anxiety goes, become as secular almost as if I had married. The one thing I ask of him is to shield me from the extreme force of this trial; and the only explanation I can suggest to myself why he does not do so is that I have in some way or other greatly offended him. And, when I cry out to you, it is not in complaint, but as signifying inarticulately feelings which are too deep for words. Please God, and I hope not from pride, I will be faithful to St. Philip, and then God will reward me, though St. Philip does not. And I will therefore bottle up my thoughts and fancy St. Philip saying to me what a French *conducteur* once did, when I was looking after the safety of my luggage. 'It is my business, not yours.'"

When we read such utterances as these and remember that they came from a mature man of great intellect and high spirituality — from a man, too, who was born and bred an Anglican, and in his early ministry was wont to make much of the reticence and reserve of our Lord and of the whole New Testament in all such matters — it almost seems as if Newman, in his Roman Catholic days, got finally into much the same state of mind as Count von Hoensbroech describes when telling of his boyhood in his Junker home in Germany, where he and his playfellows entered with gusto into the "Mass-game":[1]

"We boys were very early taught to 'minister' at the daily Mass in our chapel. . . . Only those who know the theatrical nature

---

[1] "Fourteen Years a Jesuit," by Count von Hoensbroech. Vol. I., pp. 22-23. Translation by Alice Zimmern. Cassell & Co., New York, 1911.

of the ceremony, with all its minutiæ, its liturgical utensils and vestments, its prayers, recited now loudly, now in undertones, its gleam of tapers and ringing of bells, its mystical culmination in the transformation of bread and wine into the body and blood of Christ, can realize the impression it makes on the minds of children who actually participate in the celebration. But even this participation in the Mass did not suffice for my mother. One Christmas we received as a present a 'Mass-game,' consisting of all the objects required for the celebration — an altar, vestments, missal, and all the utensils — chalice, wine and water cans, candlesticks and bell, which enabled us children to celebrate the Mass in play, and occasionally to add to it a sermon. Even our sisters put on the vestments, and, contrary to all discipline and dogma, said Mass and preached, in spite of the exhortation *Mulier taceat in ecclesia.* If other children came to visit us, we entertained them with a solemn service, and choral High Mass, when our juvenile vivacity often led to drastic scenes between the officiating priests and the faithful congregation. As this 'Mass-game' was not specially made for us, but was to be had by purchasing, it is probable that it is still played in many an ultramontane household. Conceive of it: the very culmination of the Catholic religion, around which, in the words of theologians, all else revolves 'as around the sun,' the fearful mystery (*tremendum mysterium*), at whose celebration 'worshipping angels attend,' is turned into a children's game!"

In a letter to the Duke of Norfolk,[1] Newman remarks, "The Rock of St. Peter on its summit enjoys a pure and serene atmosphere, but there is a great deal of Roman *malaria* at the foot of it." Had not the malaria got hold of Newman when he wrote such passages as those above quoted, or as the following to Dr. Pusey? Think of it, in a letter to Dr. Pusey, whom, in the "Apologia," he described as ὁ Μέγας!

---
[1] Vol. II., p. 404.

"So far concerning the Blessed Virgin.[1] And now, when I could wish to proceed, she seems to stop all controversy, for the Feast of her Immaculate Conception is upon us. . . . May that bright and gentle Lady *overcome you with her sweetness.*"

Does it not — to use Newman's own remark to Pusey about Images and some Romanist expressions concerning the Saints and Mariolatry — does not this phrase of Newman to Pusey seem "like a bad dream"? Truly, Newman is now quite as much of a distressing puzzle to ourselves, as he was in other matters to his Roman Catholic associates.

IV

We have, as far as in us lies, answered in regard to Newman all save one of the

---

[1] Vol. II., p. 108.

questions with which this study began. It remains to consider what the ultimate secret was of Newman's influence over his contemporaries who were religiously disposed. For such persons the Evangelical Movement had already accomplished much, rendering their religion serious and intensely personal, and kindling a new missionary zeal. Newman himself owed much to the Evangelicals; but Newman and the Tractarians had something else to contribute to the religious life of the Church of England, namely, their emphasis on the note of Catholicity; their interest in ecclesiastical antiquities; their wider literary culture; and above all their keener apprehension of the common social and sacramental life of Christians as members of the one Body whose head is Christ. Dean Church bears emphatic witness to this side of Newman's influence, as well as to the impression of what sainthood signifies, which Newman and the other authors of the "Lyra Apostolica" revived in England.

But besides all this, Newman had a different and weighty message for all persons who were religiously disposed, no matter what their ecclesiastical connection. We have to remember that for two centuries there has been among civilized mankind a noticeable change in the consciousness of certitude; or possibly it would be more exact to say that there has been a change in men's idea of the range of human certitude and the direction in which our sense of certitude applies itself.[1] For a considerable period previous to Newman, and throughout his time, the human intellect was chiefly engaged, and very

---

[1] Cf. Richard Holt Hutton's essay on "Religious Uncertainty."

seriously engaged, with the surface of life, rather than with the springs of life. Under the auspices of natural science a new range of wholesome and unselfish interests had been called to man's attention in connection with physical objects; and these interests had a certain largeness and catholicity and unmistakable value, though there was hardly a vestige in them of deep spirituality. Although untainted by direct moral danger, these interests manifested small promise of spiritual help. While not, in the conventional sense, "worldly," they were not "unworldly." Or, to put it differently, a new world of the superficial understanding was so occupying mankind, that they gave up the quest of the spirit. If God was not denied, He was not generally "in all the thoughts" of such men. Hereby it followed that men took most of their tests of certainty from a region which is physical rather than spiritual, and meanwhile a shadow was cast over the true spirit of man: his spiritual occupation was gone; and he was less and less aware, not only of religious certainty on his own part, but of the quality and cogency of religious certitude in comparison with the certitude of physical science.

Now it was Newman's function to reclaim spirituality for the human understanding, and to compel men to recognize that there is actuality in our religious certitude, no less than in other kinds of certitude. In this regard those who caught the contagion of Newman's personality found — at least in the sermons of his Anglican period — the tone and teaching of the New Testament about certainty in religion restored to them. During this period of his career Newman's tone was the tone of Jesus Christ. Newman *saw* Christ vivid in the New Testament, and he helped us to see Him. He made Christ a character as real to us as it is superhuman. The reasonableness, the authority, the beauty and joy and pathos, and the awful risks and prospects of man's hidden religious life were by Newman rendered once more vital to many men who, though not ignoble, had of late been occupied with the surfaces of things. The Rev. Mr. Campbell, of London, in a sermon to Presbyterians in New York last winter, said: "Ever since I was a boy I have had the feeling that the spiritual world is so real to me that I can almost put my fist into it." Newman had the same feeling, and wherever he was he made multitudes feel as he did: they renewed their hold on the world behind the veil, and the term "real" was no longer a superficial term for them, with materialistic connotation. Students of natural science expressed themselves with less aversion to the idea that "the spirit of man is the candle of the Lord," and that ultimate reality is not to be confined in terms of matter. Speaking of the lives of the saints, Newman observed:[1] "The exhibition of a person, his thoughts, his words, his acts, his trials, his features, his beginnings, his growth, his end, have a charm to everyone; and where he is a saint, they have a divine influence and persuasion, a power of exercising and eliciting the latent elements of divine grace in individual readers, as no other reading can." Newman himself exhibited sainthood to all who came within his reach. Withal, as he remarked in his sermon on "The Parting of Friends," he had a marvellous

[1] Vol. I., p. 207.

insight into the workings of the human mind and will; he read men to themselves, and comforted them in the reading, and brought to bear on them his own overmastering desire for holiness, without which no man shall see God. Like the Psalmist he had the genius to put in well-pruned words the intuitions of the spirit — the indefinite, subtle sentiments that pierce the soul and render it athirst for God. As Richard Holt Hutton observes in his essay on "The Spiritual Fatigue of the World," "Christianity cannot be understood in any degree without being approached with a certain passion both of hope and fear. The whole history which led up to it, the whole history which has flowed forth from it, has been a history of spiritual passion, and there is no meaning in Christianity at all if it be not true that divine passion is as deeply rooted in the eternal spirit as infinite reason itself." This is what Newman signified when he chose for his motto the saying of Augustine, "Heart speaks to heart" (*Cor ad cor loquitur*). Scott Holland alludes to this when he speaks of the "lyrical cry" in Newman; and Father Ryder "remembers hearing an eccentric but acute critic, with something of Mr. Swinburne's turn for grouping poets, thus deliver himself in our common room: 'Under the head Poets of Passion I would put Lord Byron, Charles Wesley and' — bowing to Father Newman — 'if I may be allowed to say so, your Reverence.' We were all very much amused, but I have often thought since that the criticism was almost as true as it was grotesque."

Thus our study of Newman ends, as it began, with the settled impression that

Newman's own intimate description of himself to Sister Maria Pia was accurate: "Like St. Gregory Nazianzen, I like going on my own way." And the clue to his whole strange course was, in large measure, his native independence coupled with his artistic temperament. He was noble and disinterested, and he worked for love; but he wanted recognition and human sympathy; and for lack of these he drooped, and seemed at last like a brilliant being chloroformed. Those of us who believe ourselves to be both Catholic and Protestant — or, as Dr. Muhlenberg used to phrase it, those who are Evangelical Catholics — cannot but commiserate Newman as he finished his Roman Catholic career, when we compare him with the Newman who had inspired and helped us in his earlier Anglican days. I have said that Newman's life was a drama, but not a tragedy; and this I think is so, if one looks at the benefits which Newman brought to the piety of individuals, and at his influence in deepening the attachment of churchmen to their Church throughout the Anglican communion. But if, on the other hand, we have regard to Newman as a personal phenomenon — to the condition of the man himself at the close of his career, as contrasted with the beginning — then we feel that Newman's life was indeed tragical. Take, for example, first the Parochial Sermons of the Anglican period; and next, the Apologia; and lastly, the occasional sermons which he published during his Roman Catholic period. In the first, as previously remarked, Jesus Christ stands out to us somewhat as He does in the New Testament — a vivid Person, a real, sufficient revelation in human form of the Heavenly Father. The immediate, accessible actuality of Christ, as the New Testament portrays Him, is uppermost in Newman's mind, and he applies it to our heart and mind and will in a most solemn and searching way. At the next stage of Newman's career, in the Apologia, Christ seems to have withdrawn into the background, and He is to a large extent left out of the argument. In the third stage the situation is even worse, for in the place that Christ used to occupy other figures have intruded — the Virgin Mary and St. Philip Neri and St. Bridget, and such like. By way of definite instance I will give that mentioned in the striking autobiography entitled "A Soul's Pilgrimage."[1] Dr. Charles F. B. Miel narrates the disappointment with which

---

[1] "A Soul's Pilgrimage," by Charles F. B. Miel, D.D., p. 48. Jacobs, Philadelphia, 1899.

he heard Newman preach at the Oratory in London on Holy Thursday. The topic of Newman's sermon was the Eucharist. "Every one was prepared for a great utterance in keeping with the day and the solemn subject of the discourse. I, for one, was disappointed. For the preacher, in giving a description of the circumstances connected with the Last Supper, chose to portray it, not according to the Gospels, but according to the revelation of St. Bridget! In the most serious manner the form of the table was described, the place which each of the disciples occupied, the shape and position of the dishes and vases, etc., etc., and all this detail was told in the confident manner of one who was narrating historic facts." To one who knows what Newman's genius and scholarship had been, and how rare his power to enlighten and pierce and elevate the human soul — surely to such this sermon in the Oratory presents the last act of a tragedy.

Yet in the case of persons who in real life have influenced us greatly, we do not strike a balance between their excellencies and their defects: we are attracted or repelled by the assembled qualities as a living whole; and if, on the whole, the influence is good, then the weight of the entire personality is imparted to such goodness. So with Newman, the final, prevailing impression that we carry from his life is, his intense personal piety combined with genuine distinction of mind and spirit. These qualities enabled him to exercise his extraordinary influence in our Anglican communion, and far beyond. They linger with us still while we sing his hymn, "Lead, kindly Light," — that intimate revelation of an earnest soul which seems like an echo of the prayer with which Petrarch closed his 'Secretum': "May God lead me safe and whole out of so many crooked ways; that I may follow the Voice that calls me; that I may raise up no cloud of dust before my eyes; and with my mind calmed down and at peace, I may hear the world grow still and silent, and the winds of adversity die away."

In order that Newman himself may strike that note for me, in closing this study of his character I quote a passage from the "Dream of Gerontius," a poem so dear to General Gordon that he carried it with him even at Khartoum.[1] Gordon's was an individuality as unique as Newman's, though in a different way, and quite as independent. Gordon, like Newman and St. Paul, "died daily"; and

---

[1] Wilfred Ward's "Biography of Newman," Vol. II., p. 515.

Newman's poem gave true expression to Gordon's martial soul. Now that both of them — the soldier and the Cardinal — have gone to their last account, we can link them in this passage, where Gerontius tells of the feeling with which the departing soul passes into the presence of his Judge and Saviour:

Soul.

"I go before my Judge. Ah! . . ."

Angel.

". . . Praise to His Name!
The eager spirit has started from my hold,
And, with intemperate energy of love,
Flies to the dear feet of Emmanuel:
But, ere it reach them, the keen sanctity,
With which its effluence, like a glory, clothes
And circles round the Crucified, has seized,
And scorch'd, and shrivell'd it; and now it lies
Passive and still before the awful Throne.

O happy, suffering soul! for it is safe,
Consumed, yet quicken'd, by the glance of God."

Soul.

"Take me away, and in the lowest deep
There let me be. . . .
There will I sing, and soothe my stricken breast,
Which ne'er can cease
To throb, and pine, and languish, till possest
Of its Sole Peace.
There will I sing my absent Lord and Love —
Take me away,
That sooner I may rise, and go above,
And see Him in the truth of everlasting day."

BISHOP DOANE—THE POET

BISHOP DOANE—THE POET

IN this issue the *Churchman* contains a letter expressive of the sincere sympathy which all friends of the Bishop of Albany are feeling at this time — sympathy which surely is shared by church people generally, for Bishop Doane is known and honoured throughout our country, and far beyond. This is neither the place nor the time to say more on that intimate theme; but I think that even here and now something can be said which will not be out of harmony with what so many of us are thinking in our hearts.

More than a generation ago the first Bishop Doane, of New Jersey, in one of the valuable footnotes to his (first) American edition of Keble's Christian Year, in quoting one of Dr. Croswell's fugitive poems, said of that notable Boston clergyman, "He has more unwritten poetry in him than any man I know." That remark might well be applied to the second Bishop Doane, and I have so thought of it lately. Standing before us, as he now does, in noble loneliness, bereaved of his last child, the many friends of the Bishop of Albany are thinking of him not so much as the Pastor, the Bishop, the statesman, the fearless leader of men — in all which characters he has been distinguished during his long career — but rather in a more pathetic guise, which appeals directly to our most human sympathies; and it is in this connection that Bishop Doane's poetic gift has been recalled to me.

If he had not spent himself in countless other ways, for the Church and for the world at large, there can be little doubt that he would have been widely recognized as a true poet; whereas in the stress and complexity of his regular duties he has been, for the most part, obliged to live "with all the music in him still unsung." Now and then, indeed, fugitive verses from his pen have got before the public, but they were inadequate samples of his unwritten store; although in his sermons and letters, and above all in his remarkable extempore addresses, there were abundant signs of his poetic cast of mind. Once or twice he has accomplished the difficult feat of composing a really great hymn, such as "Ancient of Days," which has a permanent place, not only in our own Hymnal, but in collections of sacred song put forth by other Christian denominations, both here and abroad. I recollected this hymn when, in a private letter, I was told of the touching appearance of the aged Bishop as Celebrant at Holy Communion in his little church at Northeast Harbor, about the time when the funeral car was bearing the remains of his beloved child to her distant grave.

Since then I have called to mind another poem of his, less widely known — a very human document, bearing also characteristic marks of the devout divine. Bishop Doane has always been as fond of animals as of mankind; and those who are familiar with Dr. Brown's "Rab and his Friends" and Matthew Arnold's "Geist" will find much of the fine feeling and poetry of the Scotch physician and the English man-of-letters condensed in these beautiful verses of our American Bishop, along with notes that are quite his own. For years I have had these verses on a card that stands on my study mantelpiece, to catch my eye in vacant moments. I reproduce them here as a fair example of the wealth of "unwritten poetry" that is, and always has been, in the Bishop of Albany. Possibly in this hour of deep sorrow, when his closest friends can but offer him the mute condolence of clasped hands and wistful eyes, he will not refuse to accept, from one less intimate, this earlier utterance of himself to himself, which expresses much that he has been used to say to others in like case; for here he says all that can be said, and better than others could say it:

BISHOP DOANE ON HIS DOG

"I am quite sure he thinks that I am God —
 Since he is God on whom each one depends
 For life, and all things that his bounty sends —
 My dear old dog, most constant of all friends;
 Not quick to mind, but quicker far than I
 To Him whom God I know and own: his eye
 Deep brown and liquid, watches for my nod;
 He is more patient underneath the rod
 Than I, when God His wise corrections sends.
 He looks love at me deep as words e'er spake:
 And from me never crumb nor sup will take

But he wags thanks with his most vocal tail:
And when some crashing noise wakes all his fear,
He is content and quiet if I am near,
Secure that my protection will prevail.
So, faithful, mindful, thankful, trustful, he
Tells me what I unto my God should be."

AN EXPERIMENT IN CONSERVATIVE REVISION OF THE NEW TESTAMENT

A REVIEW

AN EXPERIMENT IN CONSERVATIVE REVISION OF THE NEW TESTAMENT[1]

DEAN BEECHING, of Norwich, and Archdeacon Westcott have just published a tentative revision of the Authorized Version of the Epistle to the Hebrews; and my friend Dean Beeching, in presenting me with a copy, writes me that the authors "would be interested to know how it strikes American opinion." I am in hopes that this review will elicit some expressions of such opinion, both from Biblical scholars and from devout readers generally; since it is for the latter that this version is specially intended. The authors modestly call themselves "Two Clerks."

---

[1] *The Epistle to the Hebrews:* An Experiment in Conservative Revision. By Two Clerks. Cambridge University Press, 1912.

This revision is a result of the memorial presented last year to the Archbishop of Canterbury by a deputation headed by Bishop Boyd Carpenter and the Dean of Norwich. The memorial was extensively signed by English scholars of all denominations. It invited the Archbishop to appoint a Committee to correct the Authorized Version of the New Testament "in those places where it is erroneous or misleading or obscure." Archbishop Davidson, in his reply, expressed a wish that the memorialists should provide a specimen to exhibit the kind of revision which they desired, and he suggested the Epistle to the Hebrews as the specimen to be undertaken.

In the Note prefixed to their work the revisers state that "this revision of the A. V. is intended to be strictly conservative. Alterations are made only where mistranslation or needless ambiguity or considerations of text appear to call for them. Further, as a general principle, changes are made most sparingly in the most familiar passages. At this late hour, when the revision of King James has won for itself acceptance with the whole English-speaking race, we are convinced that if changes are to be made in what have become 'household words,' they must be such as would generally escape the untrained reader's notice. Happily it is the best known passages that least require alteration. In regard to the rest we have not bound ourselves by any rule. Aorists, wherever they come, are treated on their merits; and we have allowed ourselves much liberty in the rendering of any given Greek word. The punctuation has been freely modified, and so has the use of italics. It is only irritating to have 'is' or 'are' printed in italics, when they are not expressed in the Greek, because it is not Greek usage so to do."

It is to be hoped that the *Churchman* will in due time supply its readers with a critique of this work from the standpoint of accurate Greek scholarship; and then, of course, the question of the most authoritative texts will come up, though this question has evidently not been shirked by the Two Clerks. This present review is but preliminary, by way of calling attention to an important publication. So far as our branch of the Church in America is concerned, it has for some time been apparent that our congregations do not desire that the R. V. should be considered to be, on the whole, more than an experiment. They do not wish it to be substituted altogether for the A. V., which unsurpassed example of style is still felt to be more inspiring in worship than any other for the English race. Our General Convention authorized for alternative use in our churches an edition of the A. V. which embodies in the margin the alternative readings of the Westminster or American editions of the R. V., together with others adopted by our own special Committee for the Apocrypha. Subsequently our General Convention extended the permission, so that now the English or American R. V. may, like the Marginal Readings Bible, be used as a substitute for the King James Version in reading the Lessons in church. Now comes this new revision of the Epistle to the Hebrews by Two Clerks, as part of a movement to provide the Church of England also with an alternative to the A. V. which will be generally acceptable for use in Church services. Hereby it appears that the struggle which went on so long in England before the King James Version at last prevailed, is now being repeated. And as in Jerome's day with the Vulgate, and at the Reformation with the King James Bible, so now, the people generally, not merely scholars, must decide. Hitherto in England, as among ourselves, the R. V. has hardly got beyond the use of scholars. In public parochial worship of the Church of England it has been unauthorized and seldom read. Especially in the New Testament the authors of the R. V. were too meticulous, seeming to be fond of alteration for its own sake; as when, for example, they changed 'foreasmuch then' into 'since then,' and 'boldly' into 'with boldness.' These are but two of almost countless instances. Thus the occasional pedantry, the excessive literalness, the halting diction, the frequent failure to perceive the difference between a commentary and a vivid, vital rendering in another tongue "understanded of the people" — these qualities, over and above the novelty of the R. V., have stood in the way of its general acceptance, in spite of its many improvements and indispensable corrections of wrong translation. Ordinary readers and hearers missed the rhythm and the style of the familiar A. V., while the obvious faults of the R. V. prevented such readers and hearers from recognizing their debt of gratitude to modern scholarship. Nevertheless discriminating readers, among the laity as well as the clergy, have become more and more impatient of the inaccuracies and obscurities of the King James Bible. It is felt that we owe it to our own sense of reverence for Holy Scripture that the original meaning should be conveyed to us in a form that is more entirely worthy and intelligible.

The authors of this new version of the Epistle to the Hebrews are accomplished scholars, and Dean Beeching's other publications have already manifested a fine feeling for rhythm and the best English style. Whether the Two Clerks, in their sample of what might be done with the whole New Testament for congregational use, have accomplished the extremely difficult feat of safeguarding the indispensable good points of the R. V. while preserving the music and the majesty of the A. V., they now leave to be decided by the Christian public at large. Devout and educated worshippers should make a careful and sympathetic comparison, and give this work a fair trial. Undoubtedly the Two Clerks have properly swept away a large part of the vexatious trifles of the

R. V. which I have above referred to; yet I confess that I do not think they have quite escaped the same fault. For example, what is the vital difference between 'by whom' and 'through whom'? or between 'being made' and 'having become'? or between 'have by inheritance obtained' and 'have inherited'? Yet for myself, I am disposed to say that if I had to choose between this and the King James and the Revised Version for use at present in our public services, I should on the whole prefer this "Revision by Two Clerks"; for here the changes which accurate scholarship requires are more generally not worded so as to irritate the ordinary reader, who will often, however, be thankful that he can now understand passages which hitherto were obscure to him. The slight changes in punctuation and the occasional use of brackets are very helpful;

the marginal notes and footnotes are illuminating; and between the lines of the brief appendices scholars will discern accomplished learning and patient endeavor to weigh every side of complicated questions, although, for the sake of conservatism and popular acceptance, the A. V. has been allowed to stand except in flagrant instances. Notice in the Appendix the terse discussion as to the relative merits of the words Covenant and Testament in the difficult passage, Hebrews ix. 15 ff.; and in reference to ii. 5, the significant substitution of the words 'which is our theme' for 'whereof we speak'; and the suggestion that the phrase 'world to come' may mean 'the not yet created world' (the world in which man is living here and now), i.e. 'the New Age initiated by Christ,' as suggested in the margin of vi. 5.

As examples of the version proper, notice the bright light which is thrown on the uncertain passage, ii. 9, by the simple transposition of a comma, together with the substitution of the words 'because of' for the words 'for the.' In iii. 1, how admirable is the change of the words 'High Priest of our profession' into 'High Priest whom we profess.' How satisfying is the exchange of 'that speaketh better than that of Abel' for 'more eloquent than Abel.' Throughout chapter vi are numerous instances of slight but subtle alterations, now of a word and now of punctuation, which enhance the translation without spoiling the diction. Some of the emendations, as in ix. 11, are supported by the R. V.; while in xi. 13 the Two Clerks have, I think, improved on the improvement of the R. V.; and in xi. 17, the alteration of 'offered' to 'was ready to offer' is notable, and certainly agrees with the Old Testament story which the author of this Epistle is referring to. But in xii. 5, I cannot but think that the whole argument shows that the translation of the R. V. is right, while that of the Two Clerks is wrong. Perhaps no better example of the success of the Two Clerks, as compared with the R. V., can be found than in the respective versions of xi. 1, which I put side by side.

Revised Version	Two Clerks
Now faith is the assurance of things hoped for, the proving of things not seen. For therein the elders had witness borne to them. By faith, etc.	Now faith is the substance of things hoped for, the proving of things not seen. It was by it the elders obtained a good report. Through faith, etc.

I have chosen this particular verse because it enables me to call attention to an evident slip; for Dean Beeching writes me that 'It was by it' should read 'By it.' For purposes of comparison I select one more passage, ii. 16, where the Authorized Version reads: 'For verily he took not on *him the nature of* angels; but he took on *him* the seed of Abraham.'

Revised Version	Two Clerks
For verily not of angels doth he take hold, but he taketh hold of the seed of Abraham.	For verily he taketh not angels for his, but he taketh the seed of Abraham.

Here the R. V. renders the original more exactly than either the Two Clerks or the A. V. Few words have been more disputed by commentators than ἐπιλαμβάνεται here. But when all is said, can we do better than to borrow from Bishop Andrewes (Sermons, Vol. I, pp. 1-12)? "He taketh not the Angels'; but the seed of Abraham he taketh." Side by side with which Andrewes puts the Vulgate: "*Nunquam enim Angelos apprehendit, sed semen Abrahae apprehendit*"; and gives the gloss: "laying fast hold, and seizing surely on him. So two things it supposeth: 1. a flight of the one, and 2. a hot pursuit of the other." And another commentator interprets it: "He doth not lay hold of Angels, etc., i.e. to lift them up." But I am digressing.

By following the R. V. in the substitution of the word 'erring' for 'gone out of the way,' the thorough English of the A. V. is lost, and I miss the familiar allusion to pathetic passages in the Psalms and the Prophets. And I sometimes regret that the Two Clerks did not boldly introduce in the text of their version emendations which they have relegated to the margin. For example, in v. 7, 'save him from death' might well be '*release* him from death'; in v. 10, '*called* of God' might well be '*hailed* of God'; in vi. 1 '*principles* of the doctrine of Christ' might well be '*rudiments*'; or why not have it 'first principles,' as the R. V. does, and as, in v. 12, both the R. V. and the A. V. agree in doing? Surely this would make the intention of the original clearer to ordinary readers. For the same reason, in the translation '*leaving* the principles of the doctrine of Christ,' I wish that the Two Clerks had adopted the R. V., '*cease to speak of* the principles,' etc.; for the original justifies this, and who wants any Christian, adult though he be, to *leave* the first principles of Christ's doctrine? though a teacher may well, for the moment, cease to speak of them, and go on.

So far I have given instances of the minute criticism and comparison to which this valuable work must necessarily be subjected, after the three versions before us have first been read through as a whole, if possible aloud. It may be noticed that on page 19, in the footnote to chapter vii.

27, the Two Clerks' comment is so condensed as not to be quite clear; and on page 10, in the margin of ii. 16, the word *not* appears to be lacking; and on page 13, in the margin of verse 7, 'appoint' should evidently read 'appointeth.'

I sincerely regret that the Two Clerks have not divided the Epistle into paragraphs as well as into verses. In the R. V. the paragraphs are boldly indicated. Doubtless the verses have become so inwrought into our habits of recollection and devotion that earnest Christians would deplore any edition of the Bible for popular use which did not indicate the verses as sharply as is done in this version of the Two Clerks, and also in the A. V.; yet I cannot but feel that the paragraphs should also be given, as in the R. V. Nor do I see why both ends might not be accomplished by printing the verses as the A. V. and the Two Clerks print them, while at the same time indicating the paragraphs by clear division, leaving a blank line between them. Just as the chapters often obscure the connection of the thought, so also throughout the Bible, and above all in the New Testament, it is difficult — even for an attentive scholar, and much more for an ordinary reader — to grasp the sequence of the thought without the assistance of proper paragraphs.

Exigencies of space forbid my going through the whole Epistle so as to exhibit the loving thoroughness of touch and insight which the Two Clerks manifest throughout. Although their work has of necessity been largely negative, there is positive proof in it that a "conservative revision" of the Authorized Version is not only desirable but practicable; nor have the Two Clerks magnified their office in the objectionable way that many of the first supporters of the Revised Version did. Thus on the whole I think that the object of these present revisers is attained: that, if the whole New Testament could be so handled, the Church of England would have arrived at a Via Media between the A. V. and the R. V. which would be generally acceptable to the English-speaking world, bringing the people closer than hitherto to the mind of the original, which we venerate as God's Word.

"GENERAL" BOOTH

"GENERAL" BOOTH

He was called "General" for short. His original and proper title was "General Superintendent of the Salvation Army," but his simple associates could not away with a title in so many words, so they called him "General," and let it go at that. And this true history of the name he bore is typical of his whole career: it was a natural evolution.

The secular newspapers have given amply the details of his life, so it is needless to repeat them here; but a representative Church newspaper would be unworthy of itself if it allowed his death to pass unnoticed. Many of the methods and much of the manners of General Booth were not ours; but he had a great deal to teach our Church, and some of it has evidently been learned, both by our clergymen and our laymen. Through evil report and good report, and in spite of much physical disability, he slowly came into his own. To one who is aware of his beginnings and life-long limitations, it seems almost grotesque that staid, conservative Oxford — so jealous of her learning, so hearty in her abhorrence of "the Philistines" — should have conferred on this man her degree of Doctor of Civil Law; but Oxford did it, and Booth deserved it. For into the very heart of Oxford, and of all decent England, Booth had driven his own conviction that the most venerable of human laws are but a dead letter, unless and until they are suffused and applied by the higher law of love. All over the world there are thousands of well-to-do people who owe it to General Booth, and his blatant, conspicuous reminders, that they did not quite forget "Who is my Neighbor." All over the world there are hundreds of thousands of unfortunates who owe it to Booth, and his strange, penetrating ways, that the reality of the Christ life was brought home to their faith. And anyone who has studied Professor William James's "Varieties of Religious Experience," knows that General Booth, for all the extravagance of his expressions and the uncouthness of his ways, stood upon a by no means contemptible part of the bed-rock of human experience. And if he was to obey his Master, going into the highways and hedges to compel men to come in: if his message was to reach and seize outrageous people of the slums — not here and there a few, but thousands of them — who shall say that General Booth's methods were not necessary, at any rate if Booth, and not another, was to do the desperate business? And who but Booth did do it, or could have done it as he did?

He was a religious enthusiast, and the mystery was, that he was so marvellously practical. His long, hooked nose and Semitic head indicated his indomitable will, and should have prepared us for the singular combination in him of intrepid idealism with courage to face the facts. Far on in his career, looking backward, he declared in a moment of expansion, "I hungered for hell. I pushed into the midst of it." His way of getting there was original, unconventional to the point of repulsiveness to average Anglicans, and to average Nonconformists and Romanists as well; although Father Dolling understood him without protest; and who shall say that John Wesley, and David Livingston, and Vincent de Paul, and the great mediæval and primitive missionaries — even Paul the Apostle himself — would not have understood and approved William Booth when he made one motto out of these two: "The world for Christ," and "Soup, Soup and Salvation"? Granting that he was a pioneer in advertising and in courting publicity, can we imagine, in the face of the results, that our Saviour would not have said of Booth what He said of others who troubled His more regular disciples: "He that is not against us is for us"? True, even among Booth's most considerate critics there are many who, while rejoicing in his wonderful successes and admitting his genius, not merely for organizing men and women, but for getting men and women to organize themselves — even many such are doubtful whether his results were always economically sound or religiously quite sane. They admit his keen grasp of some of our most difficult social problems; but they are not yet sure that he solved these problems, and they fear that no successor can be found to finish what Booth began, and determine its final character. Yet what great organizer or philanthropist ever escaped just criticism in details? On the whole, the general verdict of intelligent mankind is well expressed in the letters to his family by President Taft and the King of England: "Only in the future shall we realize the good wrought by him for his fellow-creatures."

In one respect the course of the Salvation Army illustrates a tendency of religious organizations everywhere in our day. General Booth began as a Christian revivalist: the keynote of his message was personal religion; but ere long his most notable endeavours were along the lines of sociology and of experiments in social service, with religion in the background. Even at the outset of the Christian dispensation this problem came to the surface with the Twelve Apostles; and the New Testament indicates how they tried to meet it by instituting the Seven Deacons. But the problem still awaits a satisfactory solution, as our "Institutional Churches" testify. In all our Churches there are many who think that hereby the ministers of religion proper are undertaking to do directly what, so far as they are concerned, should be done indirectly: that the minister of Christ should follow more closely in the steps of Christ himself: that our ministers should inspire the motives for social service, rather than attempt to conduct it in detail. Perhaps subsequent developments of the Salvation Army, now that General Booth himself is gone, will help us all to a wise determination of this serious and complicated question.

When all has been said, how noticeably General Booth's life exemplified the truth that extremes meet! William Booth in his autocracy was intellectually at one with Rome in her autocracy. He did not want to bother others, or to be himself bothered, with questions of the intellect. Someone asked how he squared the idea of eternal punishment with his belief in God's eternal love. "What's the use," he answered impatiently, striking his hand upon the table, "what's the use of wanting to explain things, and worrying about interpretations? That's how work is stopped." He believed in educating the outcast, but he would not see that when you educate a human soul you compel it to ask questions; and that out of questions has come the spiritual stimulus which advanced the world: that even Christ declared that we must love God with all our mind, and even He confronted His disciples with a penetrating question: "What think ye of Christ? Whose Son is He? Whom say ye that I, the Son of Man, am?"

One of his latest inventions was the "Suicide Bureau," and it widens our view of him when we notice how he here combined some of the methods of the confessional and the experience meeting with those of the Charity Organization Society. Here the wretches who were contemplating suicide were induced to open their hearts and explain confidentially their misery to the captain of the bureau; and we are told that many men and women are now living steadily in self-respect and self-support, who owe their rescue to this means.

And our appreciation of him is not only widened but deepened when we read of his scheme of clubs for lonely people. "Loneliness — did you ever think," he said, "how much sorrow and wrong come from it? In the great cities there are thousands of lonely persons; not the poor, but those who have no friends or family, no place to go to where any friendly spirit may be found. I want to give them a place to go to where they may find some congenial work to do, if they so desire."

Finally, how significantly human is the fact that at the outset, when Booth was hesitating to take the great leap in the dark, it was his wife who gave him confidence to persevere.

Lightning Source UK Ltd.
Milton Keynes UK
UKHW022011071218
333658UK00009B/408/P